Junk Journal Joy

Junk Journal Joy

Find Calm and Self-Confidence
with Junk Journaling

by Francesca Radice

 mango
PUBLISHING GROUP

MIAMI

Cover Design: Elina Diaz
Cover Photo/illustration: Francesca Radice
Layout & Design: Elina Diaz
Interior Photographs: Francesca Radice

For permission requests, please contact the publisher at:
Mango Publishing Group
5966 South Dixie Highway, Suite 300
Miami, FL 33143
info@mango.bz

For special orders, quantity sales, course adoptions and corporate sales, please email the publisher at sales@mango.bz. For trade and wholesale sales, please contact Ingram Publisher Services at customer. service@ingramcontent.com or +1.800.509.4887.

Junk Journal Joy: Find Calm and Self-Confidence with Junk Journaling

Library of Congress Cataloging-in-Publication number: 2024946235
ISBN: (print) 978-1-68481-713-9, (ebook) 978-1-68481-714-6
BISAC category code: CRA046000, CRAFTS & HOBBIES / Book Printing & Binding

to my mom Wanda, my inner compass

Table of Contents

"If I can stop one heart
from breaking,
I shall not live in vain;
If I can ease one life
the aching, or cool
one pain, or
help one fainting robin
unto his nest again,
I shall not live in vain."

—Emily Dickinson

Premise

Nothing in this book is set in stone. It's my own approach. This book is the result of all the knowledge I have come across in my life about any art or craft, mixed with my academic background in psychology. Keep in mind that it's my perspective, my way of seeing and doing things. I'm sharing what's working for me right now. I invite you to take the ideas that resonate with you, and challenge yourself when they do not. Try everything, wherever it's possible. You might be surprised! I invite you to never stop questioning and learning and using your critical thinking. Most importantly, enjoy and trust yourself.

My wish is that sharing my story and all my experiences with you will provide you the same benefits that I found: healing, transformation, and a new way of being.

My hope for you is that, by helping you in this journey, you'll find your way to making your life calmer and more grounded, which, for me, is the way of joy.

Francesca Radice
Creator of *Junk Journal Joy* YouTube channel

PART 1

Starting on the Right Foot

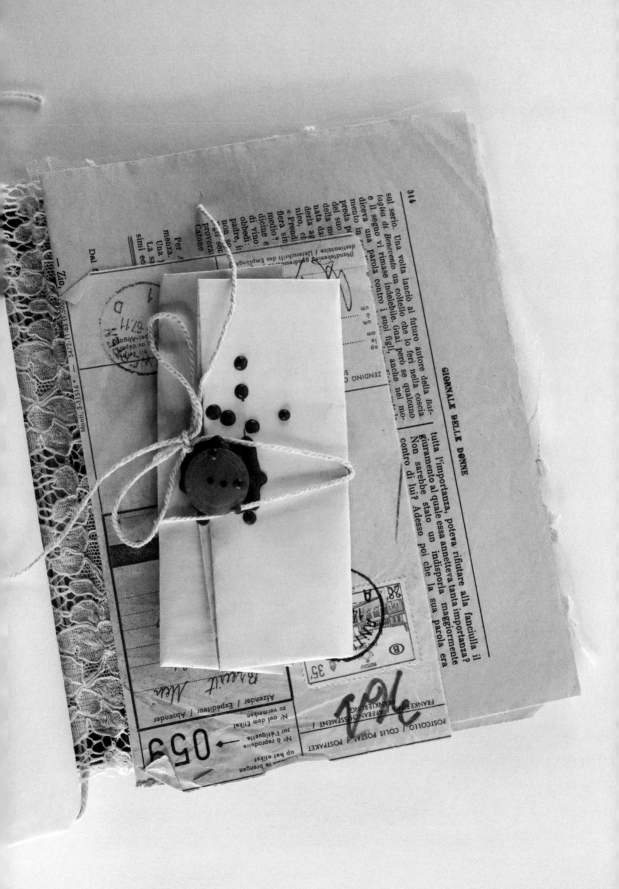

CHAPTER 1

A Promise to Your Future Self

You bought this book to find peace of mind in creating a junk journal. Congratulations! The first step is always the most difficult, and you have already done it!

Now I propose to you an exercise that in psychology is called "visualization." Professional athletics coaches, for example, use it a lot. This is a softer version, if you will, but powerful enough to trick your mind and increase your chances of getting something concrete out of this book; from creating some space for yourself to completing a whole junk journal, like the one you're reading now. Think about your big why. What do you want to achieve by using this book?

Now take a pen and a piece of paper (or use the lines below) and write as if it's three months from now and your wish has already been fulfilled. Write the specified data.

1. Where are you exactly?

   _____

   _____

2. How is your junk journal?

   _____

   _____

3. How does it make you feel to hold it in your hand? Is it soft? Is it scented? Is it heavy?

   _____

   _____

4. Does it fit in the palm of your hand, or is it chunky?

_____

_____

5. Is it full of fabric or many types of paper?

_____

_____

6. Is it very colorful, or does it have earthy colors?

_____

_____

7. Is it modern or vintage or an eclectic mix of the two?

_____

_____

8. Does it contain photos of your loved ones? Family heirlooms? Or is it your diary?

_____

_____

9. What's your journal's name? Is there a special meaning behind? Or you just enjoy the sound?

_____

_____

10. Have you gifted it to someone important who likes these things?

_____

_____

11. What emotions are you feeling?

_____

_____

12. How does it feel to flip through the pages?

_____

_____

13. How does it feel to play in it?

_____

_____

Now, imagine you're dedicating time to creating your journal with love and passion.

14. What are you doing exactly?

_____

_____

15. Where are you?

_____

_____

16. Are you in a quiet little corner in your home?

_____

_____

17. Is your cup of tea steaming near you? Or are you maybe more of a hot chocolate person?

_____

_____

18. Are you playing with paper and glue?

_____

_____

19. Are you creating with linens and embroidery pieces?

_____

_____

20. Are you enjoying yourself?

_____

_____

21. Are you relaxed?

_____

_____

22. Now, what images did you see in your head?

_____

_____

I bet you smiled.

And now, the most crucial thing. Imagine that you are your future self, the person with the most beautiful journal in your hands. What is it telling you right now? To just read this book, or to start creating something? Listen to your future self, because they want the best for you.

When you are done, take a photo of what you've written and save it as a screensaver on your phone, or hang this piece of paper on the mirror in your home, or wherever you can see it often.

When you feel discouraged (because, normally, it will happen; it happens to all of us), reread your answers. Do the exercise again.

Ask yourself:

- What would my future self tell me to do?

- To not dedicate, or to dedicate, some time for my passion?

- Does this time spent with me make me happy?

- Do I think other people will be happier too, having a more relaxed version of me around?

Your answers will be your inexhaustible source of motivation. This is your big why, why you want to do it. It's strong because it comes from within. And if you do everything with passion, if you give importance and love to every little step, every moment will be a little treasure that leads you to amazing results.

Remember that our future is nothing more than the set of little decisions that we make today. You have seen your future self doing lovely things in your imagination; now, start your day as if you are already that person. The one who loves themselves enough, who feels worthy enough, to create some space for their passion. Sometimes we forget that expression through art is part of human nature; it's necessary, right after eating and sleeping. Sometimes we think that to start something new, it has to be some kind of big revolutionary noisy act. Actually, it's stronger; it's a tiny gentle act to begin with. Can you imagine, if you create something every day, what kind of result can be yours a year from now?

Consistency is one of the keys. Compassion is the second one. When your inner critic tries to speak in your head, listen to it, thank it (yes, because it is trying to protect you from potential disappointments), and then prove it wrong!

Let's Practice

In this exercise, we'll make a vintage-style letter to help you to manifest the junk journal of your dreams. Give this experience importance, infuse it with your intention. Create some time and space to dedicate to this activity. Light a candle if you wish. Set up a peaceful cozy space. When you are ready, take three big breaths to relax yourself. Your outside world has to be quiet to allow you to listen to your inside world and your imagination.

Materials

Pen with waterproof ink
Paper, A4 size
Two cups of water
A half-cup of coffee
A teaspoon of baking soda

1. Take a piece of paper (a normal copy paper sheet in standard A4 size would be fine). Write down with a waterproof pen the answers to the questions that you read before (take your time).

2. I'm taking inspiration from a real vintage letter that I have. To reproduce the vintage look, we can fold the sheet several times.

3. Then, put it in a pot with a half-cup of coffee, two cups of water, and a teaspoon of baking soda (to remove the acidity of the coffee). Leave it for ten seconds, being sure to soak all the sheets, and then let it dry on a dish or an appropriate surface. This is the same process I use for aging some of the pages that I use in my journals, so if you are interested, keep in mind that the only difference is that I use a bigger container and two cups of tea instead of one. I don't really care about the exact recipe, because I like to be surprised by the final result. Usually, I leave all the sheets one next to another in a ventilated and dry place until they are ready.

4. Finally, when it's time, you can add a wax sigil to seal your letter. Alternatively, use some wax to glue on a button plus a ribbon that you like, or a button with strings that pass through it, to hold everything together.

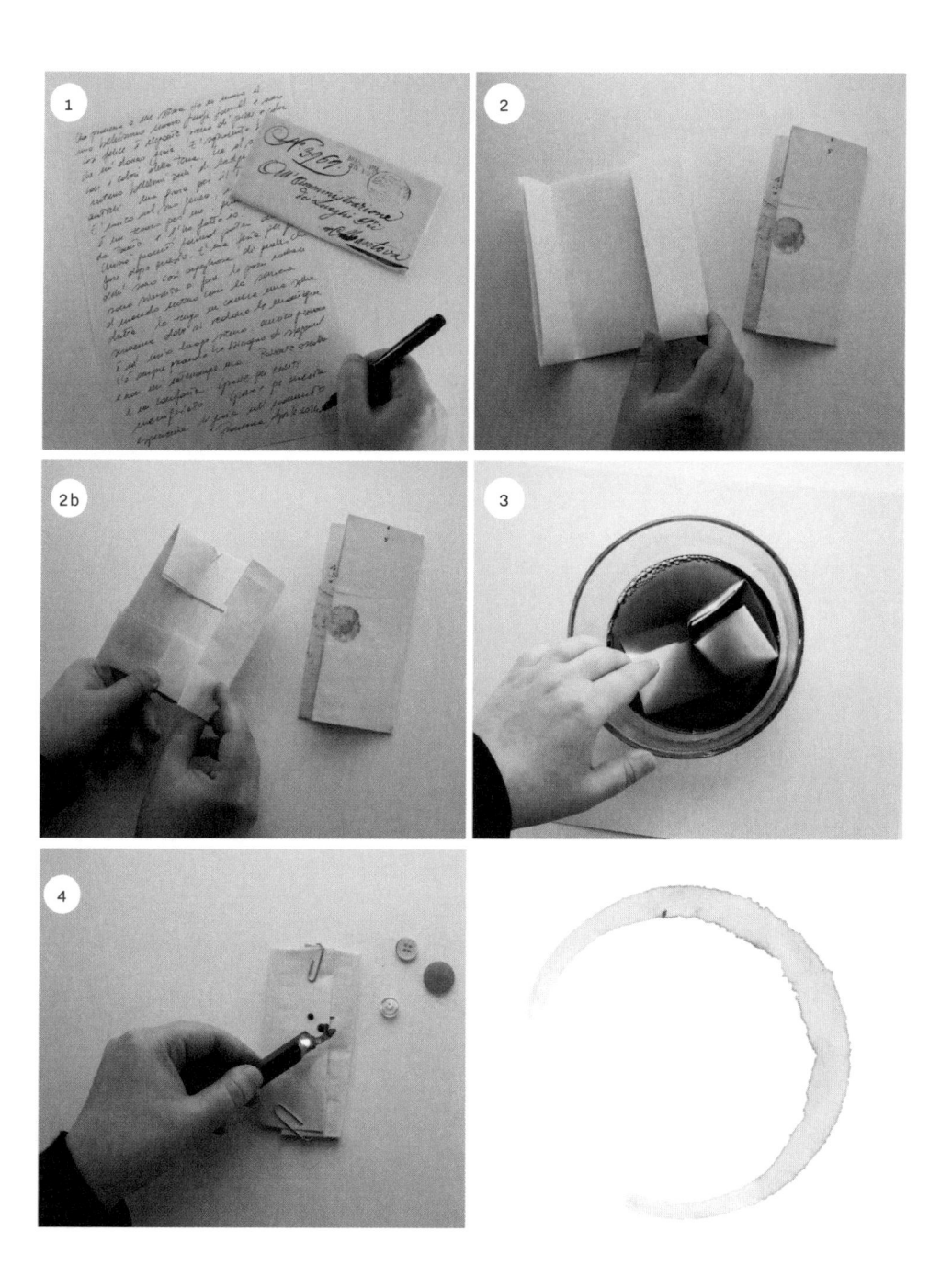

You can add this letter to your junk journal in a moment. For now, this will be your visual concrete reminder of your wish. Treasure it.

CHAPTER 2

My Story, Your Story

How and Why I Started Making Junk Journals

Imagine being able to create a beautiful handmade book with your hands out of almost nothing. Imagine being able to choose the right colors and the right materials to match. Imagine being able to transform discarded items into treasure with ease…and you want to be a part of this world.

I know the feeling; I've been there too. So grab a cup of tea and let me explain why my story is your story. Because, if you are here today, it's not a coincidence. To me, making journals is connected with my passion for journaling. In fact, when I was a little child in the '80s, I used to journal in a diary. It was a way to take stock of what happened during the day. It was mostly a way to clarify what was going on in my mind. Journaling was a way to label feelings. Giving names to emotions is a way to embrace and accept them, and learn what they have to tell us. When we listen, we can do something about it, if we have to.

It's still the same for me. When I was in my twenties in the early 2000s, journaling was a healing tool for me. It became the theme of my thesis in psychology.

At the time, I didn't know that this thing would become so important later in my life. I was thirty-three in 2012 when my mom fell ill with cancer. I advised her to keep a journal to express everything she had in her mind because I knew she would find comfort through the pages.

So she asked me to buy a vintage-style journal for that reason. Back then, she was a vintage lover, and she would love to have something special to use as a diary…but I found nothing.

So she used an ugly regular notebook as a healing journal. Writing helped her in every way possible. She was forced to live only in the now, living day by day, minute by minute. Taking notes about birds singing outside the hospital window because spring was coming, or about being grateful today because her leg was a little deflated…it was a way to find beauty and joy even in a situation like that. Because at the end of the day, we all know that it is the little mundane things that mean the most. It was difficult for me to be a powerless witness. Until she passed away.

Years passed, and then it was 2017. And every time I saw that notebook, I remembered that I had not been able to please my mother. Every time I looked at that notebook, it was 2012 again. I was powerless again.

Then, one day, I found two videos on YouTube about a strange type of journal. It was not a pompous book that seemed difficult to create, but it looked easy and fun… perfectly imperfect!

I thought: *Why not transform the old notebook into something beautiful?* It would be a great way of honoring my mother, a way to give importance and send love to her. So I did some tests, and I created my first journal. It was awful, to think about it now. Then I created a second one, and that was awful, too! But the sense of fulfillment that I felt in doing those journals was a feeling that I hadn't felt in a long time! Then I made a copy of my mom's diary, and I altered that. It was my first journal with a story to tell. That journal was not visually much better either.

But, looking at it now, it was full of meaning. Doing it was like completing a jigsaw puzzle, coming back home, a cathartic experience that helped me mourn. I closed a circle. I found peace. It broke me free; it broke the regret. This experience rewrote my story.

The thing is, creating a journal is not always a result-based experience. It's great when you create just to create, to play like a child. It can also be a way to meditate. Sometimes the meaning of it will emerge with time. Sometimes it won't. Anyway, it will be time well spent.

In 2018, I created a YouTube channel to share my art with others. I wanted to be like those inspiring ladies I saw on-screen. I thought that this would be my legacy. I failed a lot of things in my life, but I'm sure I have not failed *Junk Journal Joy*. I know that we can all contribute to the junk journal community. Today I hope my contribution includes this book. What will be yours? Isn't it magical to be a part of the same story in some way? We can all be seen and heard in this circle, like we are living in a sort of *NeverEnding Story*.

You don't have to follow rules. You don't have to be perfect. I'm not.

Perfection is boring. Our specific stories define us; let's tell them through our journals. Give love to your stories. Honor them. The more specific they are, the more universal they become. It seems a paradox, but that's the web that connects us. You already have everything you need to create; you have only to take a little step, and to begin... begin. One day, you'll pass your experience to someone else, and our deep legacy will never end.

So here's why my story is your story.

If you are reading this, it's not a coincidence.

Let's Practice

Now that I've told you my story, I want to help you to find yours with a little exercise. Why? Because human beings feel, connect, learn, and understand through narratives from the beginning of time. We come from them. We are literally made from the stories of our ancestors.

The smaller stories are, the more mundane they seem, the more actually meaningful and relatable they could be. The driving force behind all actions, the fuel, is the reason behind it, the story. Reading this book without taking action will not make you a junk journal creator, or a better one. Everything begins with an idea, and *then*, with a little step, a start in the physical reality.

So the first thing to do, as weird as it might sound, is to get a simple notebook or a sketchbook that you already have in your house, or get a cheap one from a store. Yes, in a book on how to create handmade journals, I'm telling you to get a mass-market one. There's a reason for that: this will be your companion through all this creative journey, a space to take notes, to explore through trial and error, to journal about the ugly and the weird. You can also take quick notes in the lines provided here, but if you want more space, a journal may be a better choice!

A safe space to do all the things without the pressure of matching a performance or an expectation.

Let's be real: at the beginning, we all want to create something beautiful, and if we buy a handmade journal that we like, it's difficult to experiment in it. It's intimidating. We have so much fear of messing up and ruining a precious thing that, at the end, we don't use it at all. How do I know that? Because I've been there, too, of course!

So choose your notebook: the uglier the better. Set your intention for this journal: when you use this tool, you will not know what you're doing or why, but you'll be free to make a mess.

So, block half an hour of your time in your agenda (if you can't do the exercise now), prepare yourself a cup of tea or something that you like, and answer the questions I have prepared for you. Don't rush; enjoy this time of quiet with yourself. This exercise will also help those of you who are craving to "find their own style," because nothing defines us better than our story, where we come from, why we came here in the first place.

1. What was your first encounter with the world of junk journals?

_____

_____

2. What attracted you about this world?

_____

_____

3. Do you remember the exact day?

_____

_____

4. Who inspired you and why?

_____

_____

5. Why do you admire them?

_____

_____

6. What are they doing that you can try out too?

_____

_____

7.   What values do they have that resonated with you?

_____

_____

8.   Why do you want to create a junk journal?

_____

_____

9.   What would you use it for?

_____

_____

10. Do you have, or have you had, any other creative hobbies in the past?

_____

_____

11. What do you like about them?

_____

_____

12. Why are you still doing them, or why did you quit?

_____

_____

13. Can you incorporate them in making a junk journal?

_____

_____

14. What kind of unique result could you imagine by crossing over your passions?

_____

_____

15. What story would you like to tell in creating your journal?

_____

_____

16. What do you like to preserve in your journal?

_____

_____

17. If you have already created a journal, what have you felt? Fun? Calm? Joy? Why?

_____

_____

18. What is the legacy you would like to leave?

_____

_____

19. How could making a junk journal serve you as a way to express yourself?

_____

_____

20. How could making a junk journal serve you as a way to connect with others?

_____

_____

Let's also explore what you possibly don't like, because it's not only the good things that define us, but also, for contrast, the things that we don't like:

21. What do you dislike about this world? Why?

_____

_____

22. What doesn't resonate with you? Why?

_____

_____

23. What style or approach do you dislike? Why?

_____

_____

24. What's something that you don't like and that would be challenging to try? Why?

_____

_____

25. What's the fear you have about making a junk journal?

_____

_____

26. What is this fear protecting you from?

_____

_____

27. Can you reassure this part of you by telling it that "making mistakes" is a part of the game for all of us?

_____

_____

Now get out the list of junk journal creators you like, that you wrote before, and then search for their very first posts and videos on social media, especially if they've been around for a very long time: if you are lucky, you'll find their evolution, and all of a sudden you'll realize that we all start more or less from the same place, the beginner ugly-duckling stage.

And that's it for now. These are prompts designed to create some sort of reaction, a sparkle in you; it doesn't matter that, for now, the answers will not have a cohesive meaning, or that a sort of big deep revelation will not happen.

Think of it as an exercise in stirring the waters; it will make sense at the right time. And the payoff will be huge if you allow it. Don't trust me; try it and see if it works for you.

Additional Resources

For more on starting with a clear purpose, you can read *Start with Why* by Simon Sinek, or search for his TED talk on YouTube. He talks about companies and leadership, but I think it's a concept you can apply easily in your junk journal journey. And, after all these years, his speech is still relevant, in my opinion.

Then, if you want to delve deeper into the topic of storytelling, you can read *The Hero's Journey* by Joseph Campbell and find out why all the stories have the same structure (and have fun finding yours too!).

Another very interesting model of this journey is told in *Jane Eyre's Sisters: How Women Live and Write the Heroine's Story* by Jody Gentian, where the journey is not so much about doing something spectacular, but about finding a way of living the life you truly want to have, in alignment with who you really are.

CHAPTER 3

What Is a Junk Journal nowadays?

And What's Its Purpose?

For me, a junk journal is a summary of all the things I like in one place. I've done crafts my whole life: I did crochet when I was a kid, jewelry when I was a teenager, resin art, drawings, shredding, slow stitching…anything and everything in between. I am a person who gets bored very easily, and I can't keep doing the same craft for a long time. But it's impossible to get bored when you are creating a junk journal. You can use all the skills you already have to make one: quilting and painting for the cover, resin jewelry for the tassels you can add to the spine, mixed media to decorate the pages… The type of diary you create is a reflection of who you are, a photo of an instant that represents all the skills, knowledge, and tastes that you have in that moment. Also, the physical materialization of a state of mind condensed into a book that was made by hand.

It is a mirror of yourself. There is no junk journal exactly like another.

For me, it doesn't matter what you use (which most of the time is a recycled box or an old book with tea or coffee-stained paper inside), and it doesn't matter what technique you use to make it. The most important thing is the value it has for you.

Let's be clear: there are many definitions, and mine is probably not the most "correct" or "exhaustive" you will ever hear. But that's the beauty of creativity: things are constantly evolving, and we can resist, accept, or follow our inner compass. I invite you to form your own opinion and vision of what a junk journal is. There is no junk journal police.

Let me tell you a story. I began to make journals in 2017, and in 2018 I started to share my journals on social media under the name *Junk Journal Joy*. My journals were all

37

made with cereal boxes, old and new paper that I liked, and scrapbooks or digital papers. It's still what I use now. Maybe my skills have improved and my technique has changed a little, but at the core, it's still the same.

Just a few years ago, I came across a video of a lady who was saying that a lot of us didn't make "the real" junk journals because a junk journal is made out of junk, *only* junk, and that's why the name contains the word "junk." She said she was a crafter with long experience, so she was sure of what she was talking about. So I felt stupid because I thought: *Oh my, I chose the wrong name! I'm not doing the "right" things and I'm spreading misinformation!*

Don't get me wrong, I think it is right to call things by their correct names to let us understand each other. But it is also true that there is no longer a single term of reference at this moment. We can also all agree that the initial purpose of making a junk journal was to use only waste material, in contrast to the handmade albums of the scrapbooking movement, which are decidedly made with more fancy materials.

But if the discriminating factor is that a real junk journal is made at zero cost, what then can we say about those that have a recycled base, but are created and painted with tons of expensive mixed-media paints and tools?

So I quit the discussion because, finally, I realized that it's not that important for me. When you are aware that there are a lot of opinions and no real, unique definition, you are free to decide what is a junk journal for you.

So keep in mind that what I call a "junk journal" in this book is not a "pure" junk journal. The bookmaking techniques I use are not professional ones. My journals don't fit precisely in the classic definition. If you are a little like me, maybe you've never fit perfectly in any place, just like my journals.

Do they have less value because they aren't "real"? For me, the answer is no.

And I decided not to change my social profile name. And that's because my big purpose is to transform "junk" into "joy" by making a "journal." And I'm not talking about material junk, I'm talking about the junk that we have in our head. The feelings that we have to process. Because sometimes we are happy and sometimes not, and it's proven that creativity can help us to clarify thoughts, process mess, release, and regain our calm, and our power.

I permitted myself to not fit in, and this was so freeing… Nobody has the right definition, but everybody has an opinion, so why not follow yours?

If this book is in your hand right now, it's not a coincidence, you are like me…a creative soul. You need to express what you have inside. You have this craving to create things out of nothing. And at the end of the day, this is what matters the most.

Sometimes we forget about our creative part, but it still does exist. It's a part of human nature. But we grow up and the mundane loses its magic. Or maybe we get lost because we validate the words of other people instead of our own. I'm here to help you to rediscover your path.

Let's Practice

Take some time to answer these questions:

1. What's a junk journal for you?

   _____

   _____

2. What definition have you come across that fits better with what you think?

   _____

   _____

3. What are the foundation values of this definition?

   _____

   _____

4. Why do you like it?

   _____

   _____

5. Why does it resonate with you?

   _____

   _____

6. Why do you identify yourself in it?

   _____

   _____

7. What is your ideal junk journal?

_____

_____

8. What is it made with?

_____

_____

9. What's in it? Why is it important?

_____

_____

10. Use your five senses to describe it: what are the color palettes used?

_____

_____

11. What is the perfume or smell?

_____

_____

12. How does the texture feel in your hands?

_____

_____

13. How does it sound when you touch the cover and the pages?

_____

_____

Now search for some images on the internet—on Pinterest, for example—and create a virtual vision board following all of these answers. Print the images (be sure to use them only for personal use because of the copyright), and then glue them down on the back of a recycled box or directly in your sketchbook. Add also recycled scraps of fabric, pieces of images from magazines with textures—everything that you are naturally attracted to.

Add various materials to your page, use supplies to add colors… At this stage, don't censor yourself; the weirder, the better! Act the way a child would act.

14. Do you notice some pattern?

_____

15. Is the style always vintage or always modern? Maybe a mix of the two?

_____

16. Do you imagine yourself using a big journal in your room, or a small one, maybe outside in the park?

_____

17. Is this journal made with junk?

_____

18. Are they made with real vintage things? Do they smell good?

_____

19. Do you think you prefer the ones made with digital or scrapbooking papers? A mix of them?

_____

20. With bold colors or neutral ones?

_____

21. With fabric ruffles, lace pockets, or not?

   _____

22. Does it have a soft spine or sturdy one?

   _____

23. Ask yourself, what if I change the color palette in one of those?

   _____

24. What if I change the materials used?

   _____

25. What if I add some of my other hobbies to these?

   _____

Then connect the dots: make a second vision board with all the things you find (for colors, texture, or style) and see what comes alive.

This will help you have fun discovering your taste and create a visual, cohesive, ideal junk journal that you like. And most importantly: this will help you follow…you. Art and creative things in general are always evolving, and the only rule is that there are no rules. Skills and rules are tools that have to serve you to help you express yourself better, not a cage to restrain you or make you feel ashamed because you don't follow what others think is right. As always, don't trust me; try and create your own opinion. And at the end of the day, have fun!

Additional Resources

If you are curious and you are craving to know *all* about junk journals, I mean *all* the definitions, *all* the possibilities, and mostly, how to create handmade journals with sustainable materials, I suggest you read *Treasure Bookmaking* by Natasha Marinkovic, if you haven't already. It's like an encyclopedia (but *fun*) about journal making, a book to refer to through years to come.

CHAPTER 4

The Art of Gathering

Also Known As the Art of Noticing

The art of gathering, for me, is the art of noticing. It's learning to see with the eye of a junk journal creator. Would you be surprised if I told you that you already have what you need to create a junk journal?

If you are a newbie, maybe yes.

One thing I've learned in this world is that once you start to create handmade books with all the things, you'll never look around you in the same way. You will ask yourself before throwing away anything: *Could it be useful in a junk journal? Can I make something out of this?*

One day, at a precise hour, your world will start to shift. Everything is the same and at the same time, everything is different.

You haven't gone anywhere, yet everything is new.

Because the change happened within you.

And that's why this change of perspective on things is so magical!

That's why you don't have to rush out and buy new things if you're missing something that I'm using in this book. You just have to learn to observe, think outside the box, and leave space to imagine. Stretch your imagination, and a valid substitute will appear under your nose.

The adventure starts with gathering. You may think that you will be satisfied only when you finally hold the journal in your hands. But that's not true. Once I thought the same way. I thought it was boring trying to find materials to make a journal. I was wrong. The reality is that you start creating your journal a long time before the first time you fold the pages in half. You started the moment you kept that old photo in your closet. It started when you broke that jewelry piece, but had no strength to get rid of it. It started when you collected those clothes of a loved one that didn't fit anymore. You couldn't throw away those things because they triggered a sweet memory. That's when it started.

If you have already made your first journal, or more, you know what I'm talking about.

Let's Practice

My advice for this phase is to go "shopping" around your house and pick out all those things that call your attention. All the forgotten things that are there but were forgotten and unused for a long time. Are they beautiful? Are they bringing you a memory…joy? Put everything in a basket. This will be your magic treasure hunting box.

Once you have collected a bunch of things, take your time and ask yourself:

1. Does this object remind me of something? A story? A memory?

    _____

    _____

2. Can I change the shape?

    _____

    _____

3. Can I change the color?

    _____

    _____

4. Can I assemble it into something else?

    _____

    _____

5. Take these objects one by one and turn them upside down; can you think of anything?

    _____

    _____

6. If I broke it into several pieces, could I reuse the fragments in something nicer and newer?

    _____

    _____

7. How can I make this object unique?

    _____

    _____

8. What part of this object should I let go of?

    _____

    _____

Take note of everything that appears in your mind. Make your basket dynamic:

9. Feel free to always add to or remove from it.

    _____

    _____

10. Don't save good things "for later."

    _____

    _____

11. There is no "after;" the right time is just an illusion. The only way to waste these things or regret them is not to use them at all. Each experiment will be an investment in your knowledge and will increase your creativity. There is no space for regret in this.

    _____

    _____

12. An object may wear out, but your creativity will not. It will always be present.

_____

_____

13. Don't wait until you're ready—a tiny action today is better than any long-term plan when it comes to creativity. Remember that you can always adjust your shot along the way.

_____

_____

And don't forget that it's also a great way to start decluttering what doesn't serve you anymore. You can gift some things or sell some items. The rest? Alter them and give them a new life!

Get rid of that stagnant energy! Only when you make space can the new come in.

While you are gathering things, note what you are saving and why in your sketchbook. This will save you time for a second scavenger-hunt round later. It's also important to keep track of all the ideas that come to your mind while you are collecting things in your basket because in a minute, they are gone. If you don't catch them, they could disappear, like the memory of your dreams in the early morning.

To help you, I've reported my personal list below. You can consult it, but I highly recommend creating your own because we all have different things in our house, so my list can't be exhaustive. Use my record as a starting point, as an inspiration. Don't let it limit you.

My List

copier paper

junk mail

advertising flyers

receipts

brochures

cheesecloth or gauze

sampler for choosing colors (paint factories sometimes give them away)

wrapping paper (tissue paper, colored, brown)

packaging paper

napkins

rice paper

magazines to cut out from (especially art magazines, lifestyle and interior design magazines, gardening magazines)

coupons

paper bags

candy bags

confetti bags

file folders

music sheets

ledger sheets

watercolor paper

clothes tags

business cards

thank-you cards

postcards

tickets

old unfinished notebooks

old agendas

old drawings

tissue paper

acetate (recycled from sticker packs, packaging)

glassine bags

baking paper (pieces new and the recycled ones that I use as a palette for my acrylic painting)

tea bags (used and unused)

coffee filters

wallpaper sampler (sometimes shops give them away, or you can find them in thrift stores or on eBay or Etsy) old books (encyclopedias, dictionaries, old novels, vintage school textbooks, cookbooks, gardening books, atlases, children's books, e.g., Golden Books)

playing cards

bingo cards + bingo buttons

dominoes

bottle caps

cork caps

little recycled glass bottles (for instance, I have some from hair treatment that I reused to create charms to add into my journals)

buttons (from old clothes, or find in well-stocked haberdashery shops where they are cheap)

corrugated cardboard from snack packaging

broken jewelry

charms

doilies in different materials (paper, crochet, tatting) and in different shape and sizes

old embroidered tablecloths and runners

paper clips

old keys

old belt buckles

stickers

washi tape

scrapbooking paper

vintage photos

scraps of fabric or old clothes

old bags/cases

lace, trims, ribbons

can tabs

bulb pins

sequins

light points

fake leaves

safety pins

beads

stamps

sticky labels

word stickers and/or word cutouts

pressed dried flowers

old slides

Additional Resources

I suggest you read *Little Stories of Your Life: Find Your Voice, Share Your World and Tell Your Stories* by Laura Pashby. It's full of examples and exercises to help you to recognize how enjoyable the little moments from the mundane can be. Training our capacity to notice the beauty in little things can also help us appreciate our environment more. The theme is photography and mindfulness, but the principles of this book can be easily applied when we gather materials for our junk journals.

Another great resource is the book *Make Your Own Idea Book with Arne & Carlos*, by Arne Nerjordet and Carlos Zachrison. This can help you find and see the beauty in all the pieces of paper from everyday life to make a journal full of memories and inspiration. From tickets to receipts, old drawings and magazines, and everything in between.

Finally, you can search on YouTube for the video called "John Cleese on creativity management." It's about the fact that creativity is not a talent; instead, it's the ability to play without judgments. So have fun and think outside the box. If others don't see the point of it, it's on them, not on you.

CHAPTER 5

Five Things
I Wish I Knew

Before I Started To Make Junk Journals

I'm sharing this knowledge with you because I think it can save you time in your learning process. So take advantage of my experience if this resonates with you. At the same time, take everything with a grain of salt. I don't want to limit your experience of trial and error, because at the end of the day, experimenting with all the things is fun, and with the right attitude, even the annoying ones. Despite all the preparation in this world, things will possibly go wrong, but you know what? You'll be fine anyway. Enjoy the whole package if you can. I want to just give you some starting points for reflection, not to influence you. In this way, you can see my path and think of what you want to avoid from the start; take advantage of my experience and repeat my footsteps, at least in the beginning. You are free to decide, of course. Let the fun be your compass in these types of decisions.

The first thing I wish I knew before I started to make junk journals is that using recycled packaging to create the cover is better than using one from an old book. In fact, the latter has a certain shape and size, and you have to adapt your pages and the width of the block of signatures (groups in which pages are bound to the cover) based on the length of the spine. On the contrary, using three pieces of cardboard put together (two covers and a spine) allows you to adapt it for your necessities. This is particularly helpful when you have a specific size in mind for your journal, or want to base it on the size of the paper that you are using.

The second thing I wish I knew earlier in my junk journal journey: when you choose the size of your pages *before* making the cover, you can use a page as a template to cut the others where it's needed. Then you can cut the cardboard to the same size to create the covers from scratch. You can then decide between using the same cardboard to create the spine and using something like junk mail and fabric to build something softer (we'll see this process later in the book).

Number three: If you want a flat journal that seems like a real book, you have to create and embellish the pages *before* binding them. This is a great tip to follow if you want to avoid the big chunky "crocodile" effect style (unless you like it, of course, because at the end of the day this is a matter of taste—there is no right or wrong way to do this type of thing).

Number four: The best glue to use to create a junk journal is vinyl acetate glue, because it dries fast and clear, it's strong, everything remains flat once dried, and it's good for both paper and fabrics (and for almost everything else).

Last but not least: You have to use the right thread for the binding. A wax thread or cotton thread of the right size (1 mm/0.039 in) is best because the wax on the thread creates friction and the pages stay right where they have to stay. Keep in mind that you can make your own wax thread: just pass some embroidery thread through some wax, like wax beads or wax soap, or on a candle. I want to underline that the thread has to be 1 mm size; this is important because, if it's too big, you have to use another needle that can handle it, and the holes will need to be bigger, too, due to the thicker needle. And this will cause your pages to move around in an unwanted happy dance.

Let's Practice

Learning about your preferences is a journey of never-ending discovery: keep in mind that your taste and style will change over the years, it's natural. But having some indications to recognize where you are right now will allow you to not be overwhelmed by the amount of the information out there.

So, take your vision board made in the previous exercise from chapter three and make notes on what you notice:

1. Are your ideal junk journals flat, or in a "crocodile" style?

    _____

    _____

2. What's the cover made of? An old book or something else?

    _____

    _____

3. Why do you prefer one way or another?

    _____

    _____

4. Are the pages all the same size, or different sizes?

    _____

    _____

5. Is the general look of this journal messy, or more like a real old book?

    _____

    _____

6. What will I gain from these insights?

_____

_____

7. What are the things that you wish you knew earlier in your journal making journey so far?

_____

_____

8. If my experience didn't resonate with you, why is that?

_____

_____

Create your own list in your sketchbook and make a note every time you discover something new or helpful, so you'll remember and maybe one day pass these treasured notes to someone else.

Additional Resources

For further inspiration, you can search for and watch the YouTube video "Why Keeping a Commonplace Book Will Change Your Life" by *The Daily Connoisseur*. It's not specifically about junk journals, but you can use this concept of putting together all the knowledge that you come across or that sparkles from within, your expertise, recipes, experiments related to your ideas, and what you like the most about your journey in bookmaking, all in one place: your notebook. This will be like a chronicle of your journey, very personal and specific to you.

Another one is, "How a sketchbook can change your life" by *Sketchbook Skool*, a very inspiring video about how using a cheap sketchbook to draw every day for a few minutes can improve your well-being, confidence, and skills. This video is applicable to all kinds of creativity activities, not just drawing. My two cents is to "draw your ideas" whenever they come to your mind. Don't lose them—write them down as soon as possible. When you combine words with images on paper, it's the beginning of making things real. Later in this book, I'll show you my process, but for now, let your imagination uncover what this means. It's time to stretch your fantasies. This will help you to see potential where others see things to throw away.

CHAPTER 6

How to Improve
Self-Confidence in Your Practice

Your mindset is the foundation of your creative process. If you believe that being able to create a beautiful journal is not a talent but a learning process, and a fun one, you'll do it well. If you treat your "mistakes" with a childlike approach, like what you're doing is a playful experiment, you'll enjoy every minute from the start. If during this process you treat yourself the way a good friend would, you are going to have results.

Skills will follow naturally, as I said before. But you can accelerate this process with some tips that I hope will be useful for you.

My number one tip is to play. I'm repeating myself, but for good reason: I want this to stick in your mind. Children learn through trial and error, and doing experiments. They don't fear the unknown, they are attracted by it. Observe children around you and try to remember what it was like to be one of them. We were like that naturally, and then we forgot. What did you used to do, when you were little, that you were so passionate about that time flew? Maybe you used to draw. Maybe you embroidered. Can you incorporate some of those activities into making a junk journal?

My second tip is to spend some time familiarizing yourself with the materials you gathered and your supplies. Dedicating time to them shows them love. Maybe there is something forgotten in your stash that deserves your attention. Establish a relationship with these things, bond with them. Give them names. Those supplies you bought one year ago: how is it going? Take them out and try them on that junk mail you just saved. Take care of them once you have finished, show them love. Dedication and passion is the key here. If, after six months, you didn't use them, let them go. Set them and *you* free. Make space to breathe. Giving yourself a deadline to use them will make you more committed and accountable to use or to find a better place for them.

For a long time, I didn't take care of things in general; my house was a mess, not just my craft room. At a certain point, I realized that the mess I had outside was a reflection of the mess that I had inside. So breaking this vicious circle by starting to take care of my things was taking care of myself in a certain way.

If you make dates with your art supplies to know them better, you'll nourish your relationship. You'll discover their gifts and new ways of using them. Curiosity and wonder will never disappear. And you won't need to buy new ones.

My third tip is to study your favorite artists. I mean every artist in every niche that you like. What words do they use? For instance: what are the names of their works? What story are they telling? What color combinations are present in their works? What do they make you feel when you look at their works? What could you do to bring these things into your art? Since the dawn of time, artists have learned by studying the masters. What pieces of you do you see in their works? What speaks to your soul? What emotions break through when you observe their works?

Discovering ourselves through and in the arts of others comes naturally to us. We can recognize ourselves in a poem or in a song. We can even understand a message in a collage. Without words.

Other people are able to create vehicles for expressing exactly how we feel about something through art, and what a great relief it is! When we try to do the same process, it can't be so different from the original in the very first moment, and that's alright. Creating something on our own when we are learning may entail emulating others, at the beginning.

It's like learning to write: initially, we all do the same thing. Then handwriting becomes like your fingerprints, unique. And without effort. And that's the whole point for me: don't aim to be the greatest, but the most unique. Not because it's cool, but because it means that you have accepted and expressed yourself in an authentic way. And we cannot just eat, sleep, and work; we need to express who we truly are in some way. And on a piece of paper is the safest place that I know to do it.

For me, personal style is not something to chase; it comes naturally to and from you with time. The misunderstanding about copying arrives when it comes to sharing, in my opinion. *When* and *if* you decide to show what you have done that is inspired by others, use your discernment and learn about what is allowed and what is not, and most importantly, what is fair, before sharing.

Another note: I don't know if I'm the only one who feels this way, but my impression is that we live in a world where the unspoken assumption is that, if we don't share our creations, they don't exist. If we share, we have to *perform*, or our art will be lost in the void. When we create as a hobby, at some point we feel the need to turn it into a job, or it seems like a waste of time.

Maybe you are not in this category, but if you are, here's a reminder for you (and for myself): you can create only for yourself and for no one else to see. Worthiness doesn't come from external validation, and most importantly, it doesn't depend on whether the return is *money*. Again, remember how you used to play as a child. Playing just to play, creating for the sake of creating, has intrinsic value.

My fourth tip is about the quality of your dedication in your practice. It doesn't matter if you have only five minutes a day to craft. Give those five minutes love and attention. The ironic thing is that we may think we need a whole weekend of art to create something valuable. But, instead of waiting to swim in the ocean, what is more valuable than a glass of water in the desert? It's the same glass of water that you can have right now in the coziness of your home. Maybe those five minutes are your glass of water in the desert. You have to drink it to survive. The quality of your time is more important than the quantity of time. And you can always beat quantity with consistency. A drop every day creates the sea.

Imagine creating something every day for thirty days, no matter what. In these thirty days, you'll create maybe some things that are ugly, but also some gems. If you start already knowing this truth, you'll practice with ease. Every ugly piece is bringing you closer to the beautiful one.

My fifth piece of advice is, if you already have some old work from past years, take a look at it and notice your evolution. Maybe your skills have improved, maybe you have changed style over the years. Congratulate yourself. Imagine and dream your next evolution. If you don't have some creations already, you have for sure made something else or accomplished something in some way. For example, when I was a teenager, I thought that learning to drive was impossible for me. Twenty years later I don't think that anymore. Remembering our little wins and cherishing them is always a confidence boost.

Let's Practice

Try to take some time in the early morning to do something creative—when it's quiet and your family is still sleeping. The world is still sleeping. I discovered that this time is magical; it seems like it is part of a completely different dimension. Give yourself this little time and your day will start in a different way, with a different mood. For me this works, but maybe you are more of a night owl than an early bird. Maybe for you, it's better late at night, or during your lunch break. Try it and see. You can always adjust or change.

First of all, use this time to create your portable creative kit, one that you can use in your spare time everywhere. Romanticize this time. Use a recycled tin biscuit box or a plastic container. You can use something simple or something fancy; it's up to you. Start with one that is simpler to gather and makes you feel happy to use. Give it a name. Give it importance.

Then get scissors, paper, and glue. Collect some images from magazines and some old book pages. Making collage is simple, fun, and relaxing. I think it is the most sustainable mindfulness activity. The goal here is not to create something beautiful; in this case, it's play just to play. The goal is reconnecting with your inner child.

Note every outcome that you like in your sketchbook; you'll be able to replicate your discovery in a second moment. This is very important, because you can learn from me what *I* like, what *I* discovered. But learning something *from me* will never be as enjoyable as discovering *your own* preference. Skills will follow naturally. Your style will rise naturally. And all while remembering how to enjoy the quiet in a busy world. It's giving yourself unconditional love. Give yourself love and you'll find yourself again.

CHAPTER 7

Make Challenges Your Friend

There are many types of challenges that you can do. You can decide to create a personal commitment and stick with it. Accomplishing it, even if it's "little," can give you a boost in your self-confidence because you have proven to yourself that you can trust your word. There are also "challenges" on social media that you can follow. They are designed to help everyone get inspiration and improve their skills. The goal is to follow prompts to create something, along with other like-minded creators in a niche, in a limited time period. You'll see thousands of variations of the same theme, and that will help you see things in different ways that you didn't even know were possible.

Here's what I've learned by taking part in some, and as a host of one myself.

Number one: Having a "buddy," or more than one, makes everything more fun. If it's fun, it's easier to keep going. Not only can you get inspiration and motivation seeing others doing things, but interacting with them can create connections and friendships.

Number two: If this scares you a little, it is a good sign. That's why I advise you to do it. A little discomfort in trying new things is what makes you grow. Maybe you are afraid to not do a challenge every time you should, or to not do it perfectly…so you end up not starting at all, out of fear of disappointing yourself and losing face with others. But keep in mind that you win the challenge just by trying it. That's the little secret.

Number three: If you overestimate your ability to keep going, next time, resize the challenge. At the end of the day, doing something is better than doing nothing at all. Take it as another exercise to know yourself better, to take note of what works and what does not. A challenge has to be small enough to be sustainable, but big enough to not be boring and to make you grow. But this line is different for every one of us. Only you can learn your boundaries and adjust them through action and self-reflection.

Learning about when, why, and how you do things at your best is interesting and can make your life better in general, not only in a craft challenge.

My fourth lesson is to keep in mind that, if you decide to share your journey online, yes, you are virtually in a group of people. They are watching and maybe judging you. But not as much as you may imagine. In psychology this effect is called "the spotlight effect." We tend to overestimate how much other people think about us, and so, also how much they judge us. Yes, maybe they can, but for two seconds, and then they pass onto something else. Even when they praise you. The reality is that everyone is focused on their own world. Knowing that can free you from the fear of being criticized. And what lasts forever is what you think of your craft—the rest will mostly fade away.

My fifth lesson learned is that, when you do a challenge in a limited period of time, it can lead to establishing a creative habit without thinking about it, without pressure. It's a plus; a good, unexpected consequence. To paraphrase Aristotle, what are we if not the summary of our habits? With little creative actions every day, what could result in a year?

My sixth tip is the natural extension of the previous one. Give yourself permission to create. We live in a world where actions not correlated with productivity are not considered worthy. (Truth: you are worthy regardless.) But whether or not we agree on this idea, one week has seven days; that is 168 hours. Those 168 hours consist of 10,080 minutes. What are five minutes a day just for you? Nothing. This reminder could reduce the pressure to take them. But five minutes every day, for 365 days, can make a difference in your results. Even if you want to increase your skills, or you want to just relax and enjoy your passion. Everybody knows that creating things improves well-being, right? Actually, I used to say that self-care is a "duty *and* a pleasure," because, if you don't fill your cup first, you can't pour for others. Now I prefer saying that it is not a duty at all, it's a *choice*. For me, it *needs dedication*. What is it for you?

My number seven lesson is more a reminder. When you are challenging yourself in something, try to anticipate the emotion of your accomplishment. If you imagine having a good time practicing *and* having the final result in your hand, you increase your chances of success. And this works whether your idea of success is to increase your well-being, to practice a hobby, or to have a finished journal in your hand. In case you didn't notice, this was the base of the practice for chapter one.

My number eight tip is to normalize doing "bad art." Producing "bad art" doesn't mean that you are a "bad artist." On the contrary. Be friends with your bad pieces;

the more you do them, the closer you are to a beautiful one. Ask yourself, "Why don't I like that piece? What went wrong?" In this way, every piece offers an occasion to learn something about the process. Notice also what part of the piece you *do* like instead, and why. Take the challenge like a warm-up exercise, to prepare yourself for the main event.

In this way, you will not feel pressure to be perfect, and you will get better without even noticing.

Number nine is to be kind to yourself: accept where you are and do the best you can with passion. Your art is not "no good," rather your art is not good enough *yet*.

If you start to compare yourself with others and the result is not inspiration but frustration, I have a trick for you to try. Choose some of your favorite creators and search for evidence of their journey. What I mean is that usually we see only the peak of the iceberg. We tend to assume that they are so good because they have a *natural talent*. So that's why it is important to see their beginnings. If you are lucky, you can find their old posts on social media. Notice the differences. Imagine that you are in the same situation as they were in their first post or video or whatever. Now it should be clearer that, if you want improvement, you just have to keep going. Don't compare your first project with the hundredth project of someone else.

Let's Practice

Journal about what you have read in this chapter and think about your situation. Has something resonated with you? Why? Are you thinking about joining a challenge? If so, why? What are your expectations? What do you want to achieve? Having clear intentions leads to clear actions. And this leads you to the result that you want to accomplish.

Here's a challenge that I prepared for you. I created a list of prompts to help you to strengthen your creativity and imagination. Consider that every point will make sense after a period of time. It will be like connecting the dots. Focus on every task, and the big picture will come alive with ease at some point in your journey. This will help you find what brings you joy and expand your way of creating junk journals.

You can use this list for a defined period, or in your spare time. There are fifty-two because it's the number of the weeks in a year: you can decide to take your time and dive deep and savor every sparkle of inspiration that will come up with each prompt. They are designed to be the beginning of something, so you'll expand and do your own research for more personal insights and discovery. To start, choose a day and block the time that you can dedicate to this date with your creativity. Test what works for you. Try as many prompts as you can. The most important thing is to start; an unexpected twist will follow. As the poet Robert Frost wrote, "the only way out is through." Have fun!

1. Pull out all your supplies and swatch them on recycled pieces of paper. Why did you buy them in the first place? Are you using them to their full potential? How can you have more fun using them?

2. Cut images that speak to you from magazines and create your little collection of ephemera to store in a bag, ready to use later. You can divide them by themes or colors, or create a story with them, like a photo novel. Journal about why you chose them, what it was that you were drawn to.

3. Create samples of stitching. If you are not familiar with stitching, you can discover a fascinating world on YouTube for free (just search on "basic embroidery stitches" or "slow stitching for beginners"). Journal about connections. Reflect on what this word means to you.

4. Create a sample of visible mending. If you are not familiar with what it means, you can easily learn what it's all about on YouTube for free (just search on "visible mending tutorial"). It's great to bring new life to damaged clothes, but also to create something interesting and unique in your soft-cover journals. Journal about rebirth. Reflect on what this word means to you.

5. Embroider on paper. Search the hashtag #embroideryonpaper on Instagram for inspiration. For instance, my favorite way to do it is to add a pop of color with thread on vintage black-and-white photos or postcards.

6. Cut little pieces of fabric that you like and create a little sample booklet.

7. Turn an old book into an art journal (just tear some pages and cover the others with white gesso).

8. Decorate a page in your journal with different materials in the same color.

9. Decorate a page in your journal with different materials in the same color palette.

10. Create a color wheel with different materials from your stash and add it to your journal.

11. Draw a flower with your non-dominant hand, using a pencil.

12. Copy a picture by drawing it upside down (the result might surprise you).

13. Create a textile page in your journal: use different materials with different textures.

14. Learn how to draw or paint a rose with watercolors (search on YouTube).

15. Mix acrylic yellow, cyan, and magenta to create as many colors as possible. You can also use other mediums, like gouache or watercolor. Search for "modern color theory" on YouTube if you are not familiar with color mixing. I used to think that color mixing was boring, but actually it is a very calming activity. This is kind of the apotheosis of "staying in the present moment." And at the end, you'll be surprised by how many possibilities you have just using the primary colors.

16. Mix every color you have created with different amounts of white. Note the recipe of the color you like the most in your journal.

17. Mix every color you have made with black. Note the recipe of the color you like the most in your journal.

18. Use a color palette you have never used before to create a page in your journal.

19. Combine vintage elements with modern ones.

20. Put some rice on a page and draw circles around the grains.

21. Close your eyes, put your finger somewhere on this page, and complete the prompt that comes up.

22. Sing and dance to your favorite song. Journal about how you felt.

23. Study some artists you love: what is that you like so much in their art? What color palettes do they use? What are the themes of their works? Is there something that you can try in your journal?

24. Make a series of cards at the same time. What is the most beautiful of them for you, and why? Can you replicate the result and create a recipe for it?

25. Go deep with the prompt that you like the most so far.

26. Search on Pinterest for color palettes that you like. Are they combinations of bright colors? Muted ones? Natural? Neon? Take note of what you enjoy the most.

27. Take an image you like (from a magazine or from a deck of artistic cards, for example) and discover what colors are in it. You can use an application on your phone, like "colorviewfinder" or similar, and then play with different color palette combinations. Take note of what colors you like most and why. Think about how you can use these colors in your journals. Do you have some paper or fabric in this color? If not, you can perhaps paint them.

28. Make a study of your favorite color. Search on Google for the story behind it and the meaning associated with it. Then you'll be able to use it in your journal to express something intentionally.

29. Google "hex code + [name of your favorite color]" and then enter the resulting code on the site www.colorhexa.com. Take note of the information you get. You'll be surprised by the discoveries you can have with just one click! You'll have the complementary color, analogous color, split complementary color, triadic color, tetrad color, monochromatic color, and alternatives—also shades, tints, and tone color variations. It doesn't matter if you are not familiar with this terminology right now, you can intuitively understand the meaning just by viewing the images. This is a great tool to easily understand what colors to use together when you are creating, whether it's a full journal theme or just a page in your art journal.

30. Make a study of your least favorite color following points 28 and 29. Why don't you like it? During this study, has any variation emerged that you might like?

31. Try to understand your relationship with colors after the latest exercises. You could find some interesting stories about yourself and understand yourself better. Let me explain with a personal example. As you may know, I'm a big fan of natural earthy colors. It comes easily for me to use them in my journals. I think they are soothing and calming, and that's what makes me happy right now. I seek calm and peace in the midst of a noisy world. I discovered that I don't particularly like bold colors, probably because they remind me of the '80s, when I was a child, which was not a particularly pleasant time for me. So all the fashion and design of that decade, like cluttered houses, vivid bright appearances…was too much for me. I discovered that I like what Gen Z call "grey millennial" (not in a good way, apparently). And that's so interesting to me: everything returns like a cycle. Maximalism and then minimalism, and now maximalism again. Even in the designs of journals. What you like most is something that others don't like at all, and vice versa, for different reasons. And it's okay. But anyway, it's interesting to discover what the story behind your preference is.

32. Search the meaning of your name, or of someone you love, and create a page in your journal with things that remind you of the meaning.

33. Print a black-and-white photo, and color the background with the medium that you like the most in the color that you like the most.

34. Create a page in your journal inspired by your favorite book's theme. What was the message of that story?

35. Write down your family recipe, if you have one, or your favorite dish from your childhood. Draw the final result, or search for a picture of it to add to your journal. What memories and emotions come through? What smells and tastes do you remember?

36. Replicate the most satisfying project that you ever did, but with a twist (change colors or materials, for instance).

37. Take an unfinished project and try to create something with it. Give it some love.

38. Clean your crafty space. Maybe some ideas will come up unexpectedly from nowhere while you see and touch all your supplies.

39. Observe what you did during this challenge: have you noticed a pattern? A certain color palette that you used the most? Is your work flat or full of layers? Can you recognize your signature yet? What are the things that you enjoyed doing the most? What are the emotions that you've been able to convey through a project? Take notes and journal about it. The more you learn about what you like and what you don't like, the more you will know yourself. And when you know yourself better, you can do more of what you like easily and have more fun.

40. Learn something new. Watch a tutorial on YouTube, read a guidebook. It doesn't have to be related to something strictly creative, so to speak. Learn some common sayings in a new language, for example. How we speak is how we understand the world. And knowing how other cultures see the world can expand ours. This impacts our imagination. For instance, years ago, I discovered that Eskimos have more than twenty names for snow, because for them specifying is important for their survival. Another discovery for me was the term "apricity," an English word that means "the warmth of the sun in winter." We don't have a word for that in Italian! This could be the inspiration for an art journal page for sure!

41. Recreate something that you did when you were a child and notice the differences. What has changed? Why? Can you bring something back and incorporate it into your practice?

42. Go for a walk to intentionally find beauty where you live. Take pictures or draw what you've discovered and write your feelings in your journal or sketchbook.

43. Hug a tree or walk barefoot on the grass and journal about how you feel afterward.

44. Cook something you usually buy, by yourself, from scratch. (Can you imagine the sweet aroma wafting while something delicious bakes in the oven?) Refresh your environment with some flowers that perfume the whole house. Take a picture or draw it and document the experience in your journal.

45. Use a thing in a way that it's not meant to be used (for example, use an empty toilet roll to mark a paper with some paint).

46. Search for a painting you like and discover the story behind it. Journal about the experience and incorporate a little reproduction in your journal of it.

47. Resume a game that you used to play when you were a child. How does it feel?

48. Create your little dictionary of personal symbols: do you have a special ring? Are you often attracted to the same shapes? Do you notice synchronicity around you? Recurrent dreams? Try to use them intentionally in your journal on a spread.

49. Use a deck of cards with creative prompts or with just images. From one or more of them, let your fantasy create a story to tell in your pages.

50. Rewatch one of your favorite movies of all time. Who is the character in it that you admire the most? Why? Create a page on the character, inviting those strengths into your life.

51. Notice and take notes of glimmers, the tiny moments of your mundane when you feel a rush of wonder, calm, and happiness. For example, spotting a rainbow, watching the sun rise, petting a cat, or listening to the rain… Create a spread about your experience.

52. Notice and take notes of triggers, the tiny moments of your mundane when you feel a rush of anxiety, anger, and frustration. Try to observe how you feel and where in the body this occurs. Observe your thoughts like clouds in the sky. Embrace them and then let them go. Journal about your experience.

PART 2

Projects

CHAPTER 8

How to Give a New Life to an Old Agenda

I've been creating junk journals for several years now, and I'm still so surprised by the number of items that are forgotten in a corner of my house! This time, to make this book, I performed a new round-up around my home, and I was quite sure I wouldn't find any particular item to repurpose…I was wrong! I found an old agenda of my mom's from 1989, never used (I would love to know why!). This could be a perfect base for a new journal, practical and meaningful. "Practical" because it's an old agenda and I can't use it anymore in its current state. "Meaningful" because it's not like another agenda, this is unique. This belonged to my mother.

Then I found an old blouse that I had saved from my '90s era (fun fact: it is the same blouse that Monica from the popular old sitcom *Friends* was wearing in one of the first episodes; that makes it more special because it was my favorite TV show when I was a teenager!). Caressing the fabric and feeling its texture takes me back through the years, to sweet memories.

This is the perfect example of how the art of gathering never fails to surprise—just give it a try.

While you are treasure-hunting around, remember to observe everything with the special eye of a junk journal creator. You can always come back to chapter four anytime to trigger different ideas on how to repurpose forgotten hidden gems.

Unfortunately, I can't show you the making of that particular journal (instead, I'll show you another, similar one), because I did it completely wrong! But from this I learned a lesson. You need to take test photos to make sure everything goes well *before* starting to take pictures of the project. Why? Because I had confirmation that it is impossible to replicate a junk journal like that. There is no other agenda of my mom's from 1989…there is no other t-shirt from the '90s like mine. Not because they were literally "precious," but because they were memory keepers indeed. That's the beauty of this type of book. They are precious to *us*.

Tools and Materials

old agenda or old book with a rigid cover

old lace cloth fabric (as an alternative, you can use a big doily)

scissors (or cutter/ruler)

glue (vinyl acetate glue like Fabri-Tac, Flash Bond, or Tacky Glue, glue stick)

gesso and a brush

liquid acrylic ink "raw umber" (as an alternative, you can use coffee or tea or an ink pad)

thread or ribbon that you like

Step 1: Preparing the Cover

The first thing to do is to cut out the block of pages from the cover of the book: use a box cutter and start from the top left of the spine where there is a gap. Do the same thing on the other side. Use a pair of scissors to cut the leftovers on the spine.

Step 2: Adding the Fabric

Cut a piece of the lace fabric cloth and add it to the cover. I suggest you use vinyl acetate glue and add it little by little on the part with the embroidery. If the piece of lace is bigger or smaller than the cover, all the better! Perfectionism is boring, in my opinion. Also, the effect of seeing/not seeing it and layers creates movement and catches the eye of the viewer. Being imprecise in this process is an advantage—keep this in mind.

Step 3: Preparing the Surface

If you like the colors of the book cover and the lace cloth, you can skip this passage. If you prefer to change the color and create a more cohesive look, then cover the structure with plaster. I suggest you not cover everything, especially on the corners, because it gives a "frame" effect that gives depth and harmony to your cover. You can use a large brush to spread it, and then let it dry for some hours (better overnight). Remember to put something like parchment paper underneath to avoid ruining your desk. Gesso is like a paint primer (or makeup primer) and allows the surface to become more toothy/ tacky and ideal to paint. A cheap one from the market will work just fine, for this type of work. In fact, it doesn't matter if it will leave some lumps, as they will blend with the fabric's texture.

Step 4: Painting the Cover

After the gesso is dried, you can add some splatters of coffee or tea or an acrylic liquid ink. Try to create a sort of natural splash or wave with the ink and then use a paper towel or your finger to spread the color on the cover. Don't forget to also add some ink on the edges. But I suggest that you not cover everything; this will add some movement that will attract your vision through the cover in a wonderful journey.

Step 5: Adding Final Touches to the Cover

At this stage, your cover will be a little messy, but it's okay. There is always an "ugly" intermediate phase when you are creating a journal— at least, most of the time. So don't worry if you don't like the thing right now; trust the process and simply go on. Your perseverance will be rewarded with the final result.

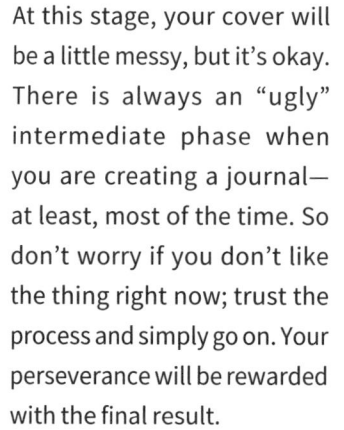

Load your brush with a little bit of gesso and gently pass it over the embroidery part of the lace. This will allow the flowers to stand out again from the background. This is important because, when you have a focal point, it's more pleasant for the eyes.

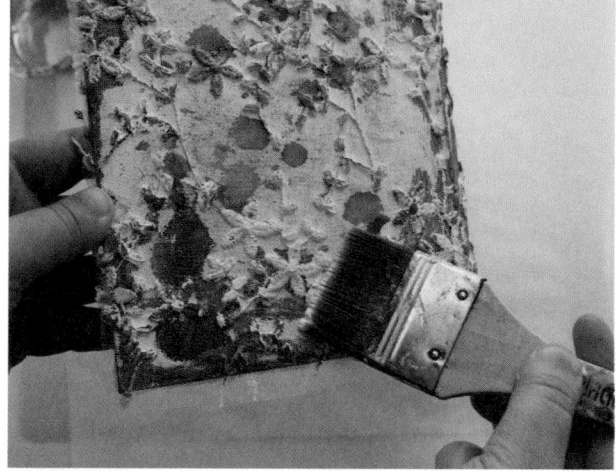

Step 6: No Sew Binding

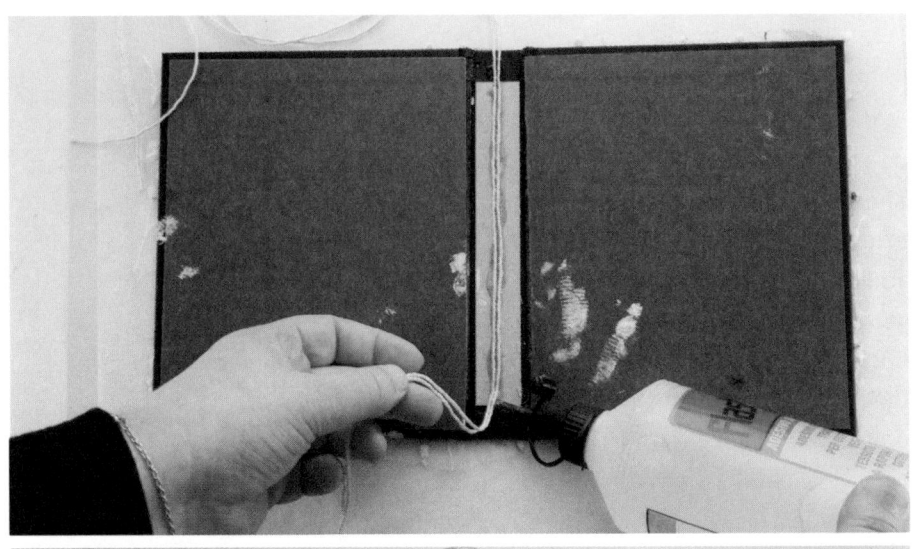

Add two strings of thread in the middle of the inside spine with some vinyl acetate glue or another type of strong glue. I'm using macrame thread, but feel free to use what you have; it's not important what the type is, as long as you like it. Be sure that your thread is long enough to hold the pages that will be added in a second moment. Keep in mind that I'm adding two strings because of the width of my spine. Two is enough for a little spine of 2 or 3 cm (0.78 in or 1.18 in). The wider your spine, the more strings I advise you to use. It's not so crucial to be precise on where to put the strings; just be sure that they are basically in the middle. If you are more comfortable in taking measurements to place your thread, feel free to use a ruler and determine it. Then glue on top of the inside spine another piece of lace and let it dry.

Step 7: Decorating the Inside Cover

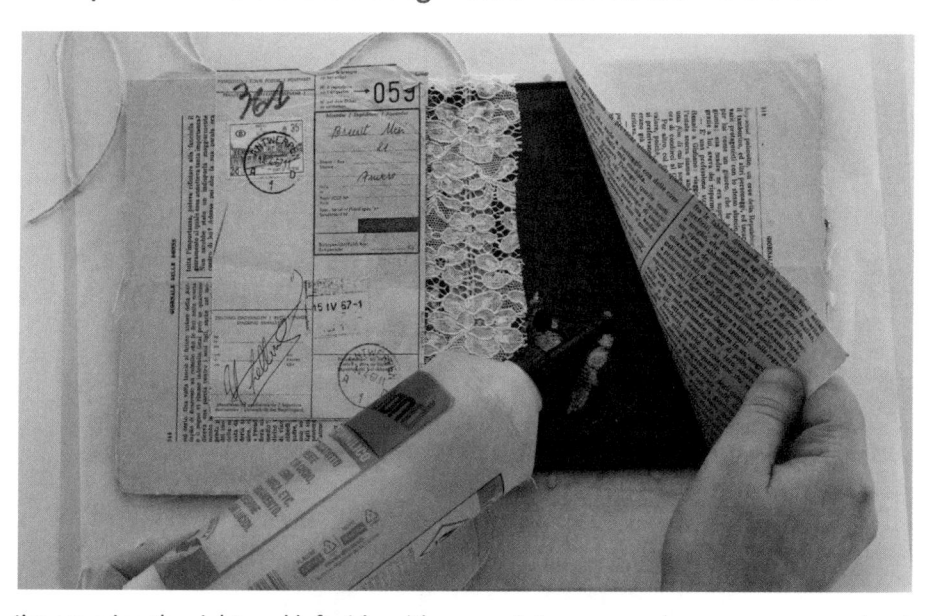

I'm covering the right and left side with some vintage pages (you can use scrapbook paper, warped paper, digital paper, book pages…whatever you have, as long as you like it).

Step 8: Adding the Pages

Add some pages that you like: I'm using some coffee-stained paper (see chapter one to see how to do them). Tie a knot to secure them to the cover. This "no binding" method is perfect when you don't have a big collection of paper or you are not so sure what to use, because you can always add or remove pages another time.

CHAPTER 9

How to Make a Junk Journal in Five Minutes

It was a cold morning in winter, 2018. I was visiting the open-air market that happens every Monday in my town. A stand full of tablecloths and runners caught my attention. I stopped to browse, and that's when I noticed a cushion cover for less than 2€! It was white and grey, very elegant, in a shabby-chic style. I held it in my hand to feel the softness. My eyes saw a pillow, but my imagination was already seeing a journal.

A sustainable one, to be precise. Affordable and quick to make. And now we'll do one like that together!

Tools and Materials

pillowcase from a thrift store or new (I got mine at a fair in my town)

three or more simple notebooks that you like

an elastic thread (or big elastics)

vinyl acetate glue like Fabri-Tac or Flash Bond

bulb pins and/or paper clips

some embellishments, like vintage postcards, tickets, and fabric that you like (mine is from the "Roxycreations" shop on Etsy)

a metal embellishment with holes, or a button

Step 1: Creating the Cover

Get some notebooks with covers you like. Three will be just fine. Fold the pillowcase in half and adjust it to the height of your pack of notebooks. In this way, you will have a sort of natural pocket on the front. For the width, fold your pillowcase around your pile and create a pocket on the inside back. Adjust until you like the result. Place the back cover of the last notebook in the fold. Hold everything together with a paper clip, or you can glue down the fold. I prefer not to, because I want to be able to extend the cover spine if I want to add some more journals in the future.

Step 2: Putting the Inserts Together

To add the other notebooks, you can just use an elastic in the middle of the last one, and then slip the other notebook from the middle into the elastic. Repeat with the third one.

Step 3: Embellishing the Cover

You can create a fabric pocket by gluing down a piece of linen on the back. To add interest, you can put something inside, like a card made with vintage office paper that peeks through. On the front, you can add a postcard and hold it with a bulb pin. On the pocket, you can add a doily, a postcard embellished with some lace, a ticket, and a vintage envelope with an embellishment in acetate. Then you can hold everything together with a clip.

If you don't have vintage things, I suggest you use images from magazines, scrapbook paper, digital images, or your photos, for example.

Step 4: Creating a Closure

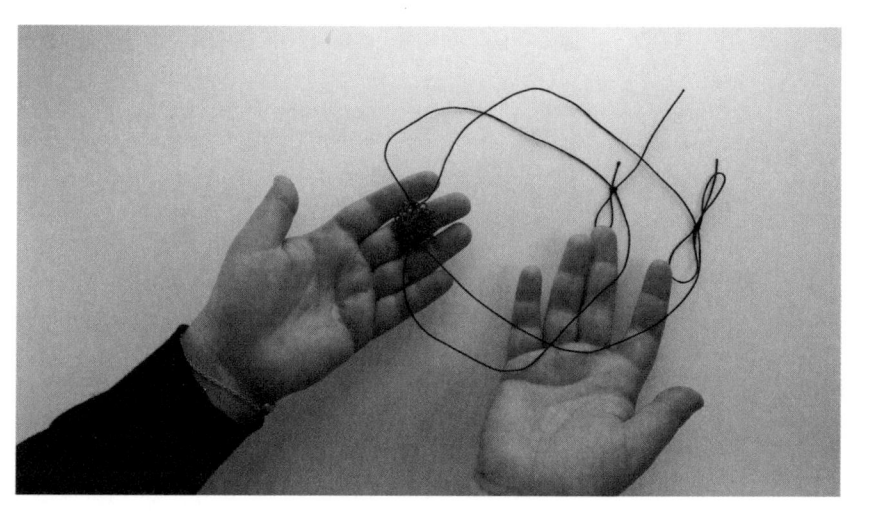

Thread two pieces of elastic (long enough to hold the journal) through the holes of the metal embellishment or the holes of a button. Tie a knot in the back of the journal, and your closure is done.

Live every day with intention

CHAPTER 10

Recycled Jeans Traveler's Junk Journal

Like many others junk journal creators, I love to repurpose a pair of jeans to create a journal. We all have some clothes that we used to dress in, but now don't have the strength to give away. So years pass and they remain forgotten in our wardrobe. What a waste…until we give them a new life! Especially when we get chills when we touch the fabric because it triggers a good memory. Sometimes this feeling is too precious to let go. Here's why I want to share with you the easiest way to create a journal with this special cloth, so it will be with you for a longer while still, and in a useful way. This version is fast to make and effortlessly chunky, a pleasure not only for the eyes but also for your hands. Have fun!

Tools and Materials

Recycled jeans (or a recycled pair of pants)
Recycled plastic placemat or recycled plastic notebook cover (the plastic nature of these things allows the structure to be flexible and at the same time strong, but if you don't have it, you can use a recycled large mailing envelope, for example)
Scissors
Fabric scraps that you like to embellish the cover
Fringed ribbon
Glue (vinyl acetate glue like Fabri-Tac or Flash Bond or Tacky Glue)
Elastic ribbon
Big needle (a needle for binding, or at least one that is stronger than normal, because denim is thick)
Buttons, can tabs, and/or metal embellishments
Photo or a tag that you like to use as a topper on your cover

Step 1: Creating the Base of the Cover

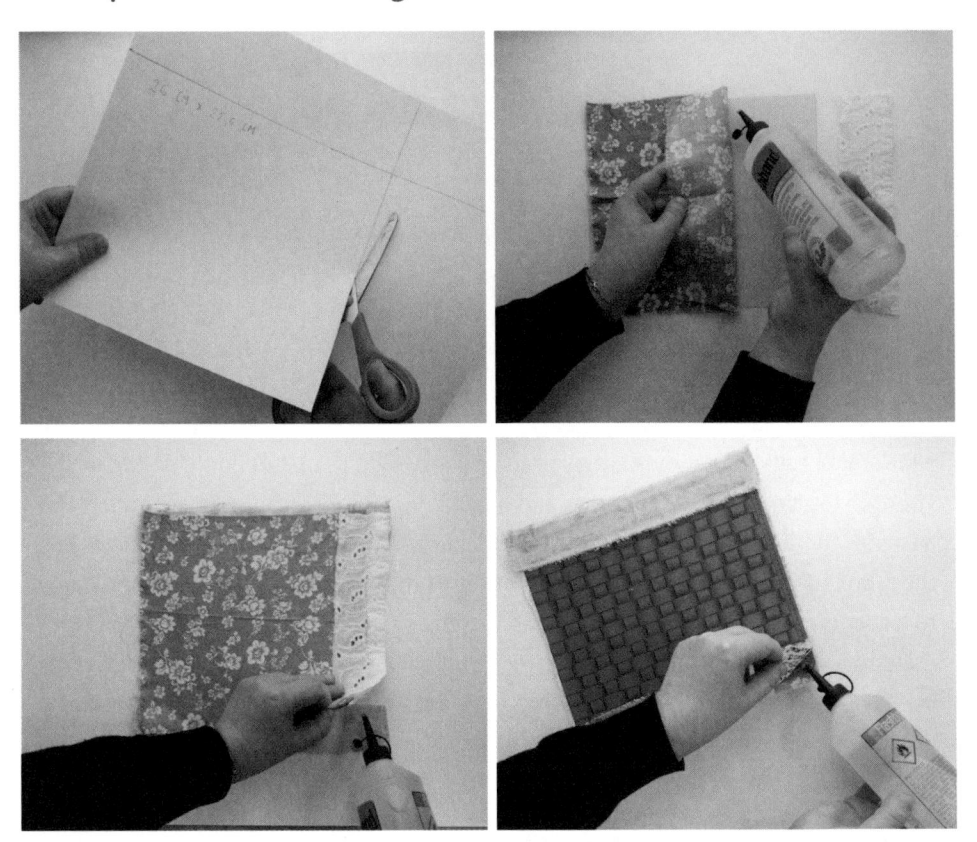

As the base of this project, you can use a recycled placemat or a plastic notebook cover. They are very strong and flexible, ideal to achieve the shape of a traveler's notebook. I chose to use a placemat because it has a sentimental value to me: I've used it for years for my breakfast! But if you don't have one, I suggest you use a large, recycled envelope from the mail instead.

Once you choose what to use, cut it with the measurements you want. In my case, I want to make a traveler's notebook, so I'll cut it with scissors in a rectangle that is 26 cm x 22.5 cm (10.2 in x 8.8 in). With this shape, you'll be able to fill your journal with two or three standard inserts at least.

Cover the inside with some fabric scraps (I'm using a piece of my mom's cloth and a fabric that I like). I'm creating a little collage because none of these is large enough to cover the inside of my base. I'm using vinyl acetate glue: I suggest you use the nozzle of the glue container to spread it well, so you'll avoid stains (especially if your fabric is thin). On the back, you can add a ribbon with fringed edges to be sure you have everything covered there, and also because I think it gives a more cohesive look to the whole.

Step 2: Creating the Base of the Cover—Part 2

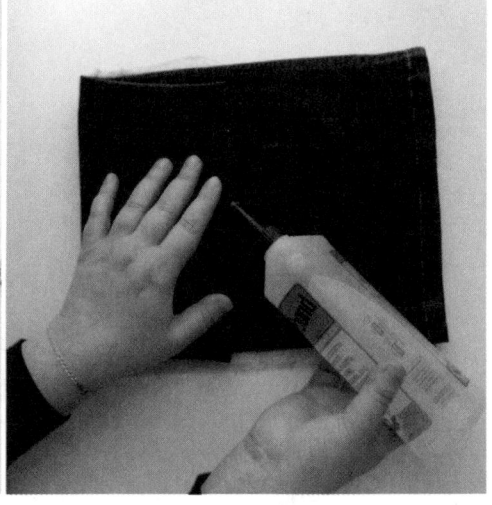

Pick an old pair of jeans—mine are from fifteen years ago, and I remember clearly when I bought them! It was such a lovely moment. I'm glad that I can give them a new life and keep them with me a little longer, given the beautiful memories they inspire. When you use something personal like an item of clothing from your wardrobe or a loved one's, it brings the best experience, in my opinion. But if you don't have something like that, or you don't want to cut your old clothes for any reason, you can find a lot in thrift stores, online or not, or ask family and friends if they have something forgotten that they can give you.

Place one of the legs of your jeans on your base and fold until you reach the middle, more or less. Cut with scissors and fold the final edge in a way that allows you to create a pocket on what will be the back of your journal. Glue it down with vinyl acetate glue (like Fabri-Tac or Flash Bond), but only the final edge, to give space for the void that will be the pocket.

The reason why I'm using the leg of the jeans without opening it is because it gives depth and strength to my cover, and the whole project will be more defined, since we are taking advantage of the sewn and finished parts of the jeans. If you want a grungier look and flat cover, cut your jeans and follow the same steps.

Step 3: Creating the Elastic Closure

This journal is quite soft, so in this case you don't need an awl to create a closure. You can use just a needle bigger than average, the one that you used for binding a hole big enough to contain the elastic thread. Put the needle in the center, more or less, and push gently. I'm not measuring, but feel free to use the ruler to determine the exact place to put your needle if this makes you feel more comfortable. For me, it's not a big deal. because I'm using a type of binding that doesn't require precision. Your elastic will hold everything together no matter what, even if it's not perfectly in the middle. Pass through the hole going from the inside to the outside and then back to the inside again. Create a loop that serves as a closure and controls the width before cutting the elastic thread and tying a knot.

Step 4: Creating the Elastic Binding

To create the elastic binding and make the holes prettier, you can use a can tab, buttons, or metal embellishments or some combination (or anything that has holes in its structure, so also embroidery or tatting embellishments). You have to make two holes on top and two on the bottom with a big needle, at least 5 mm (0.19 in) apart. You can do them horizontally or vertically; my experience is that it makes little difference. Once the elastic is the right length, it doesn't matter if the origin of it is at the same height as the insert that will be added through it. You can also use your button and/or ornaments as a template to create your holes. I suggest you don't cut the thread until the very end, so you'll be able to adjust the length and to use just the right amount.

Now pass the elastic thread starting from the inside of the cover. Now is the time to add some embellishment through your needle, from the back of it to the front and to the front from the back. Then pass it through the cover again. Go to the bottom of your inside cover and repeat the same process there. If you already have some inserts to add, try out the length and the tension of your elastic before cutting the thread and tying a knot. If you haven't, be sure to leave a generous length and not create a strong knot. This will allow you to reopen and adjust your elastic according to your needs.

Step 5: Embellishing the Cover

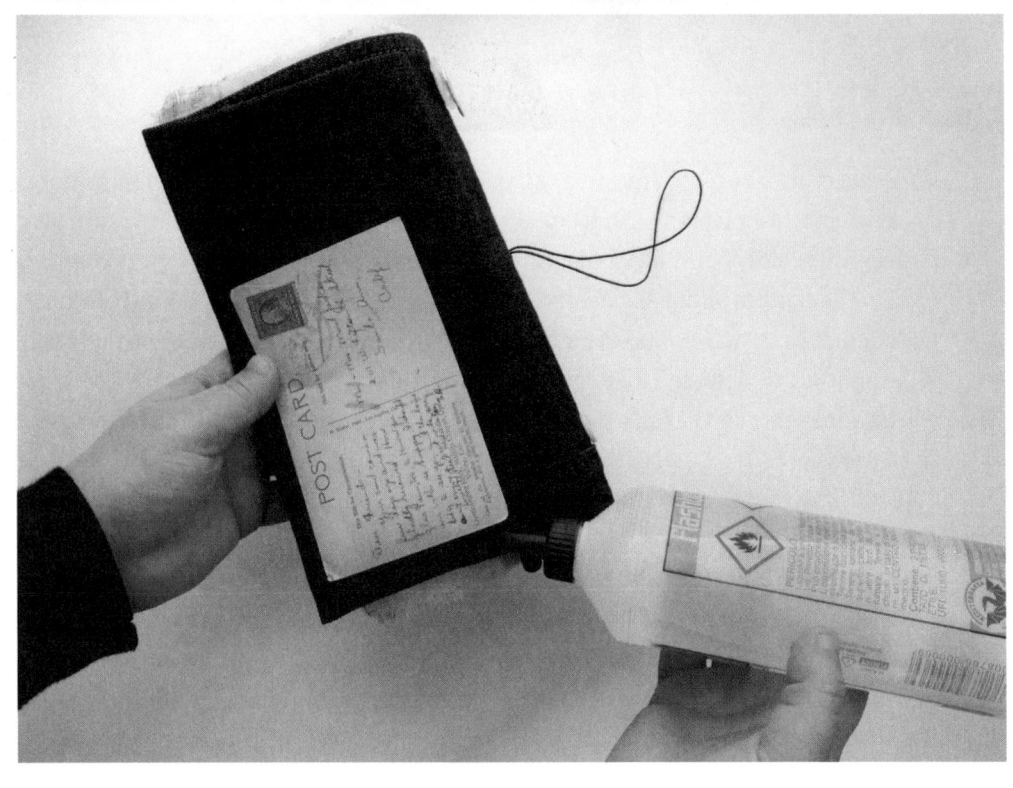

To embellish the front cover, you can make a topper, or in other words, something beautiful to place on top of it.

As a base, you can use a recycled tag cloth or similar that fits the front of your cover. Then you can layer various elements in this order: large scraps of vintage ledger paper (or scrapbook paper or digital paper or book pages); then something smaller; then a photo with a piece of beautiful fabric on top of everything. You can use glue to pull everything tighter or, like me, use the stapler and pins here and there to give more freedom to your paper: when the paper is not so tight, the light creates shadows and depth, which is something that I love so much. If you prefer something more defined and flatter, go for glue. You can use a large paper clip to add this topper to the cover (so it will be removable, and you'll be able to change it if you get bored at some point). Otherwise, you can use vinyl acetate glue to make a perfect adhesive with the denim.

CHAPTER 11

How to Create a Paper Bag Junk Journal

I'm not the only one who likes using brown lunch bags as covers to create junk journals. So maybe if you are not a total newbie in this world, you've been able to see a lot of envelope-style journals made out of them. And today I want to share with you my take on this process.

Tools and Materials

Scissors (or cutter/ruler)

Paper, 160 g/m², to print on digital images and a printer or, alternatively, use some paper that you like (scrapbooking paper, magazine pages, wrapping paper, etc.)

360-degree rotatable stapler (optional) or paper clips

Brown lunch bag for the cover

A piece of fabric that you like for the inside cover

Glue (vinyl acetate glue like Fabri-Tac or Flash Bond or Tacky Glue, or a glue stick)

Cotton thread 1 mm/0.039 in + awl + needle for the binding

Scraps of fabric for the spine + thread and needle (alternatively, a thick piece of fabric that you like)

Step 1: Creating the Signatures

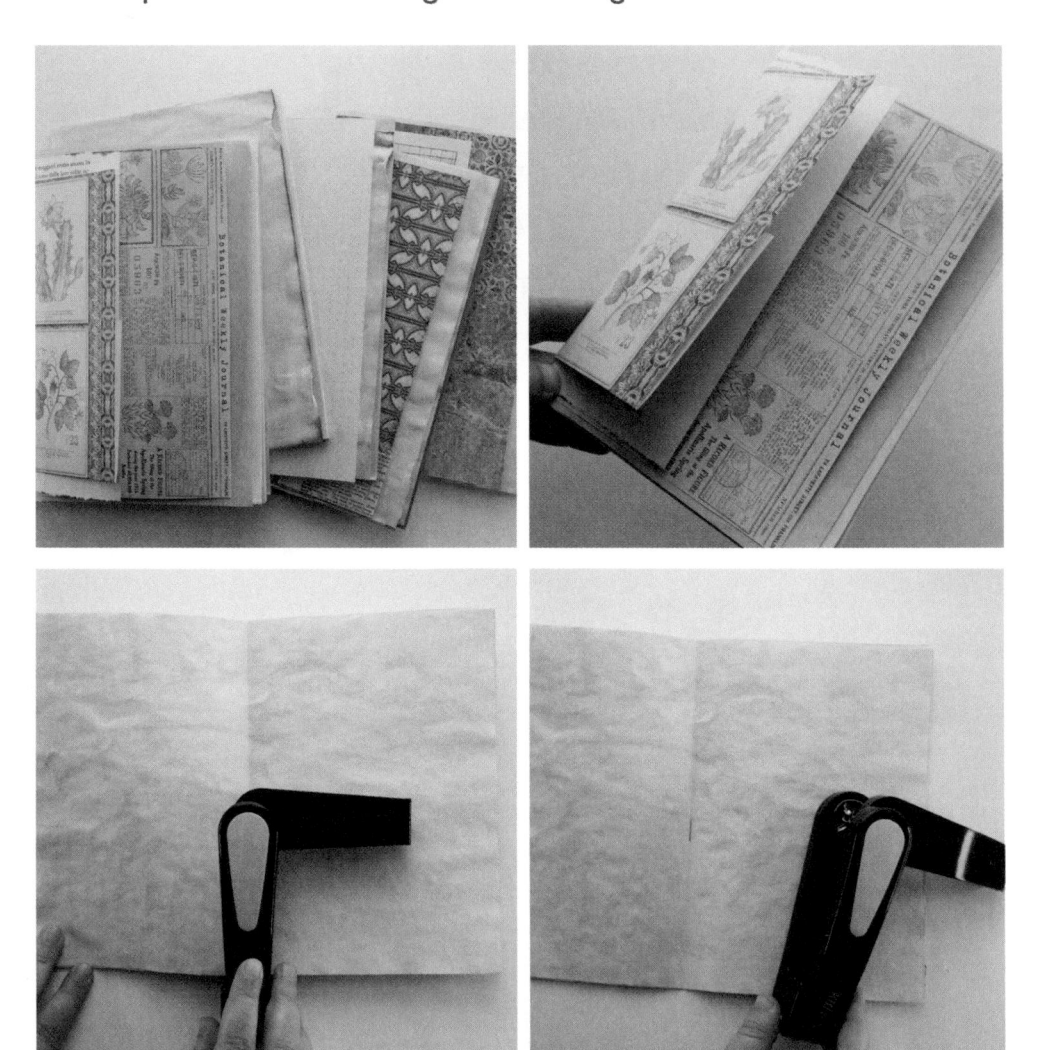

A signature is a group of pages that will be sewn together into the cover of your junk journal. For this project, you can prepare five signatures with six or seven pages of random sheets of paper that you like. For instance, you can use blank pages with shades of colors that you like and two or three pages in different sizes with patterns or images on them. For these, I'm using a mix of digital images from VectoriaDesigns and real vintage paper or book pages. Creating a sort of waterfall at the beginning of every signature is one of the easier ways to add interest to your journal. To hold the pages together before binding them, I like to use a 360-degree rotatable stapler on the center of every signature. Alternatively, some removable paper clips will work just fine. Having the pages still will make your job easier for the next steps.

Step 2: Binding the Journal to the Cover

For the cover, I decided to use a brown lunch bag because this is about the right size for the pages I have, and it's very resistant and flexible. The first thing to do is to add some fabric to the middle of the inside. This is a thing to do if you want to avoid seeing the brown of the paper when you flip through the pages, once you have set all the signatures on the cover. It's not necessary, it's up to you.

I'm using a piece of cotton, and my advice is to use something that has the same color palette as the paper that you are using. When you are in doubt, I suggest you use neutral colors, because they go well with everything. Keep in mind that, if you are using something not so thick, you have to spread the glue very well or you'll cause some unaesthetic stains. Spreading the glue with the spout of the bottle can help.

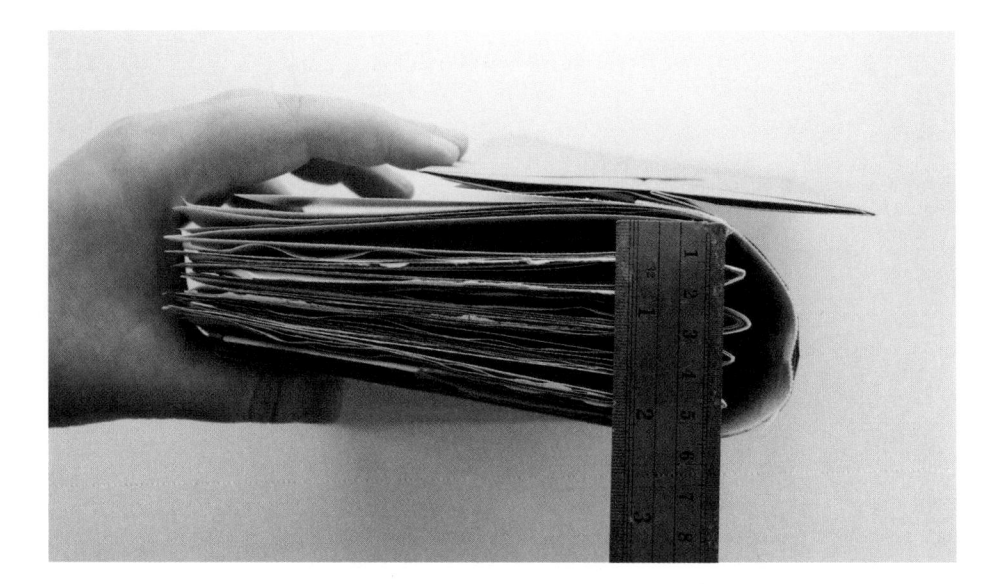

Place all the signatures in the bag, as far apart as you like, and then with a ruler see what that distance is and draw a line from the top to the bottom. When you take note of the width you like, keep in mind what you are going to do with this journal. For example, for me, it is 1 cm (0.30 in), which is enough space to add some photos or collages in the future. I suggest you try the way I do things and then see if it works for you, adjusting as desired. Mark 0.5 cm (0.19 in) from the top edges and then mark the center of every line you have made. It's not important to be accurate in placing your signature exactly in the center of the bag. That's because the edges of the cover will disappear into two pages folded in half, which will be the base of the front and back cover.

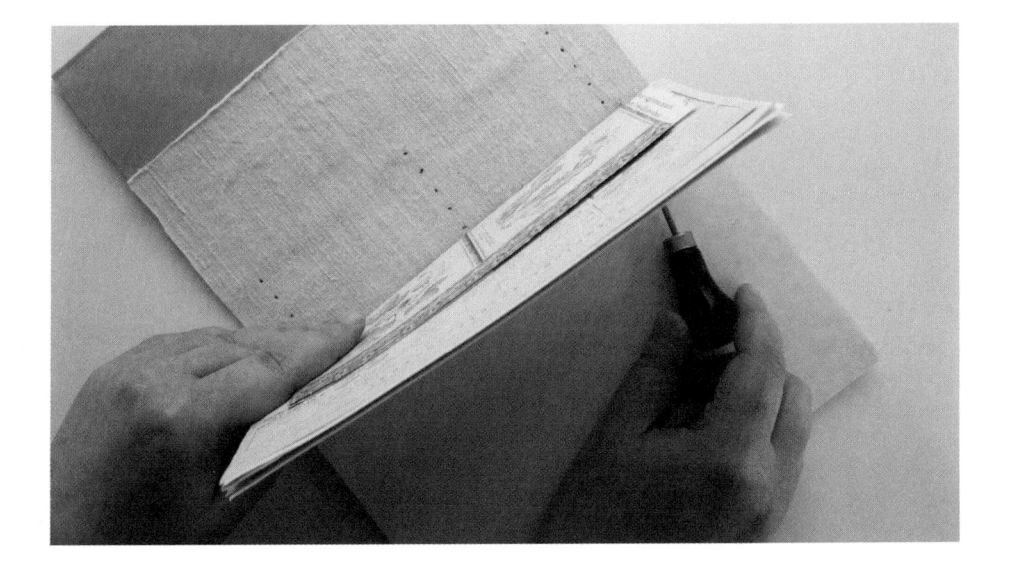

Protect your table with some cardboard and use an awl to make the holes where you have made the marks.

Hold your pages together with some paper clips, if you haven't done this yet, and then place every signature near your cover marks, so you'll have a reference for where to make holes in the pages too. If you prefer, you can mark with a pencil and then make holes, using what you did on the cover as a template. Now it's time to sew the pages to the cover.

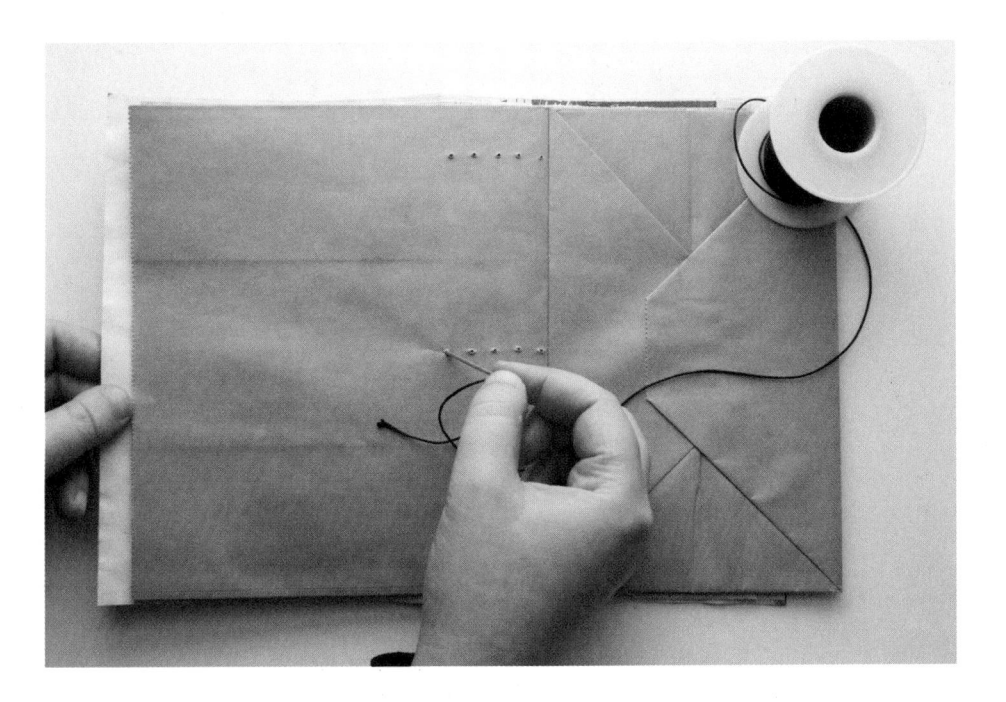

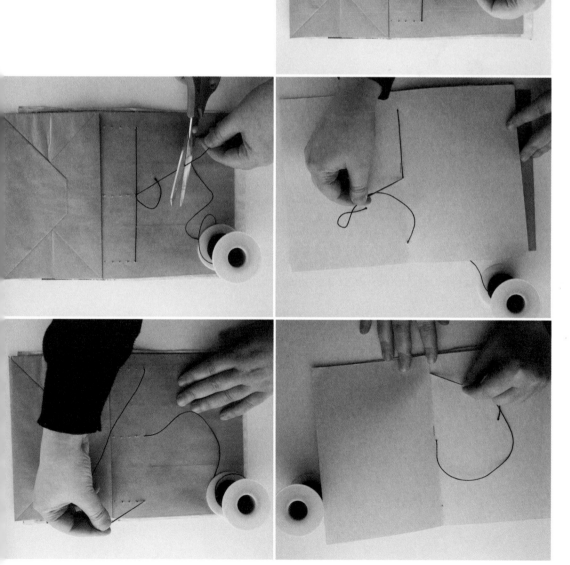

Start with the last signature (if your dominant hand is not the right one), because it's more comfortable, and use a 1 mm (0.039 in) cotton thread and a needle with a hole big enough to take the thread, but not too big (otherwise it will cause excessive widening of the holes in the pages).

Don't cut the thread; leave it in the spool until the very end, so you'll be able to adjust and use only the right amount of thread. I prefer to sew every signature individually because, if at some point I have a problem with a signature, this will not affect every other signature.

Start from the outside center of the cover and take the center of your signatures. Then go on the bottom, then on the center again, and then through the top. Check that everything is straight, adjust your thread (not too tight, not too loose), and then cut and make a knot.

Repeat this process for every signature.

→

Step 3: Finishing the Front and Back Cover

106

Glue the bottom of the bag. I didn't do that before because I wanted to be sure that eventually the binding would be finished under that. At this point you will notice that the bag is not big enough to cover all the signatures. It's not a big deal for my taste, but if you don't like it there is a simple way to avoid that. The solution is to add a page folded in half and glue it down, embracing the edges of the paper bag. You can repeat the same for the back, or create a pocket and glue that on. This way, you'll be able to still use the natural pocket of the bag and another one, depending on how you glue the page folded in half. Mine is not glued on the top, so I'll have the natural horizontal pocket of the bag plus a pocket with the opening on the top. This will create movement in the journal, and it will provide a base for other interactive elements.

Step 4: Finishing the Cover

To cover the spine, you can use a collage of fabric that you like placed on a piece of muslin or cotton. It has to be big enough, or bigger than the spine, to cover it. Use something that matches the color of the paper you already have used. My match is not perfect, but I like it anyway, maybe because the general vibe is still muted and vintage. Place your scraps intuitively, placing them in a way that makes you feel happy. But in my experience, you can't go wrong if you use some semi-transparent lace on top of everything, especially if the embroidery touches and connects different elements. If you are comfortable, use some pins to hold everything together. Then create little stitches to connect everything. The less precise, the better. It shows that the journal is handmade and unique.

Also, I can say that slow stitching is a practice very useful for relaxation. You can add some buttons, paillettes, or beads if you want. Then glue the fabric spine onto the journal.

107

CHAPTER 12

How to Create a Junk Journal

With a Semi-Exposed Soft Spine

A weakness becomes a strength in this type of journal. Usually, the cover has the function of protecting the pages beneath. So having the spine and the front and back covers at the same measurement is important because it envelopes the inside like a hug. But, on the other hand, being imprecise and embracing the wonkiness of a spine that doesn't match can lead you to create something unconventional and unique.

There are infinite ways to create what is called an exposed spine journal. My version is very beginner-friendly, and it takes advantage of something that you already have in your house for sure: an envelope. Keep in mind that you can personalize most of this basic knowledge in a moment—for example, embellishing the spine with embroidery, buttons, etc., or simply making the spine more exposed, as you wish. I'll show you when and where these variations occur.

Tools and Materials

Paper, 160 g/m^2, to print digital images and a printer or, alternatively, use some paper that you like (scrapbooking paper, magazine pages, wrapping paper, etc.)
Scissors (or cutter/ruler)
360-degree rotatable stapler (optional) or paper clips
Junk mail envelope for the spine, or corrugated paper from packaging (like the inside of a box of biscuits or crackers)
Pieces of fabric that you like to decorate the spine + tea bags
Glue (vinyl acetate glue like Fabri-Tac, Flash Bond, or Tacky Glue)
Cotton thread 1 mm (0.039 in) + awl + needle for the binding
Base for pendant
Pencil
Mod Podge (or another glue that dries clear and works like a sealer as well)
Ribbon

Step 1: Creating the Signatures

For this project, you can prepare nine groups of six or seven pages of random sheets of paper that you like, folded in half. For these I'm using a mix of digital images from Making & Creating and a mix of soft-colored papers to match the Liberty-style theme. Don't be too scared about how much writing space to leave or how many pages to use in general. Create your signatures and then adjust before the binding. But whatever you come up with, you can always add more pages using washi tape or clips, turn out pages or cover them with white gesso to be able to journal on it. You'll discover your perfect formula with time, and only by testing things. We are all different, with varying tastes and needs. So keep in mind that mine are only suggestions and starting points. Embracing the unknown is a part of the journey.

Step 2: Binding the Pages

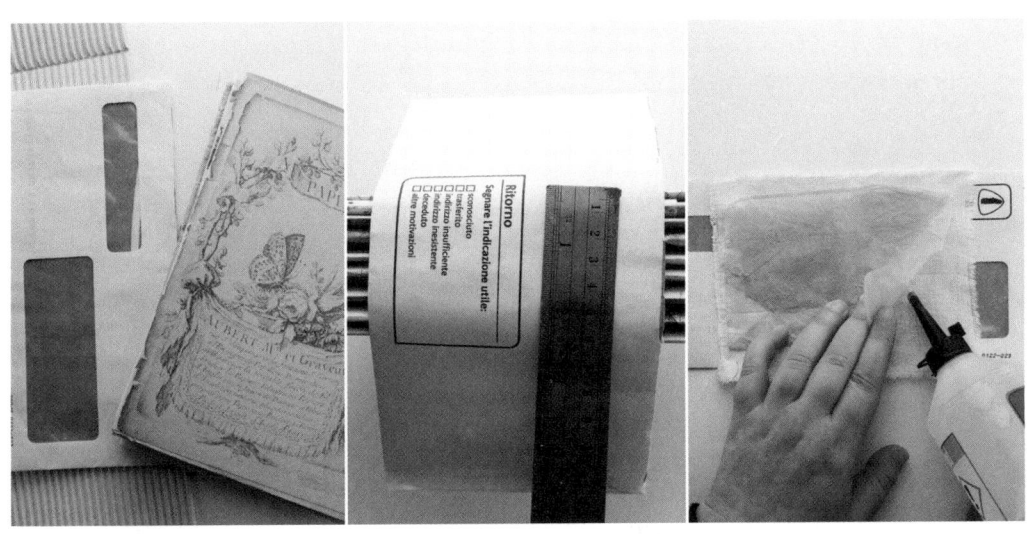

For the binding, you can use a junk mail envelope, or a piece of corrugated card stock from packaging, the kind you can find inside biscuit or cracker packs. Place the envelope horizontally on your signatures and, with a ruler, check how wide you want your spine to be. This is also the time to adjust your number of pages if the width and space of the signatures doesn't feel right to you. Also, remember that if you like to add a lot of elements and photos and things and you don't like to end up with a "crocodile style" junk journal, this is the time to add your embellishments or to keep in mind approximately how much space you need. You can use a 360-degree stapler to hold the pages together, or some clips, to make the binding easier in the next steps.

Cover the inside of the envelope with a piece of fabric, and eventually also with a tea bag for a more interesting grungy look. Then, on the front, I suggest you mark a line of 2 cm (0.8 inch) from the top and bottom edge and then mark the center. From that, mark 0.8 mm (0.3 inch) for every signature.

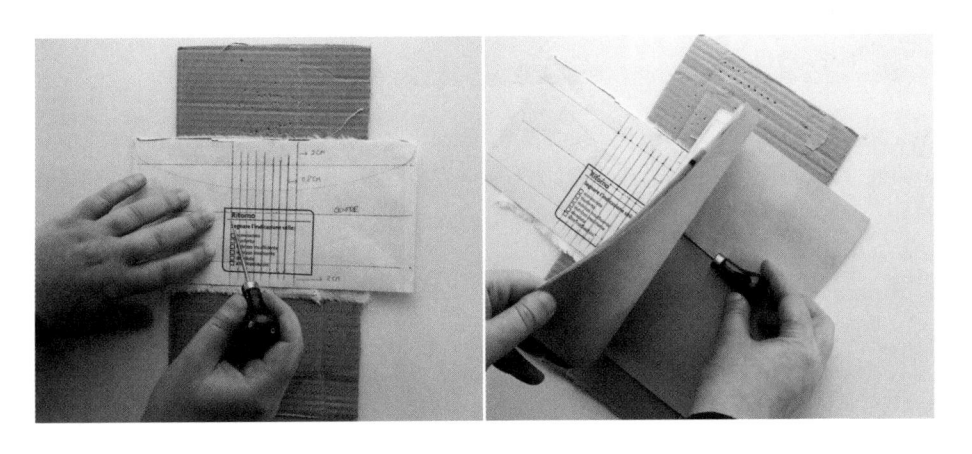

Where the lines meet, create a hole with an awl. Remember to protect your desk with cardboard on the back. To make holes also in the signatures, line them up with the center of your envelope and push the awl through the pages in alignment with the three holes made on the spine.

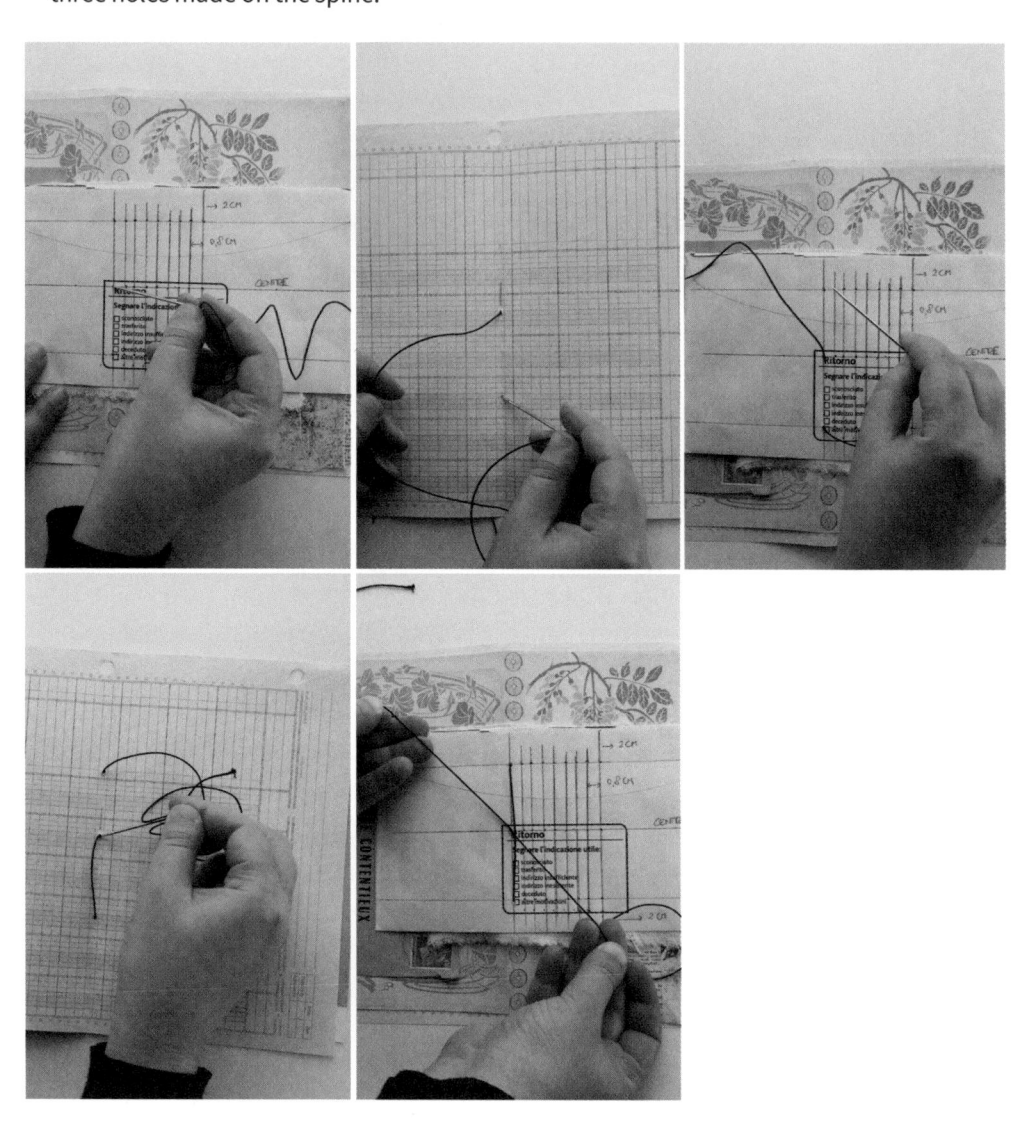

Start pulling the needle with the thread starting from the inside center of one signature. Then go to the outside bottom of the spine. Go to the top, and then again into the center. Check that everything is straight, adjust your thread (not too tight, not too loose), and then cut and make a knot. Repeat this process for every signature.

Step 3: Finishing the Front and Back Cover

Now add something special to your spine: I'm adding a tea bag and a vintage lace directly on it. You can also create a piece with special embroidery or buttons or sequins—whatever you like—and then glue it on.

Take a page folded in half and glue it on, embracing the edges of the envelope. You can repeat the same for the back, or create a pocket and glue that on as well. To make the cover stronger, you can also add a piece of cardboard in between the fold before paste them together.

Step 4: Making a Special Closure

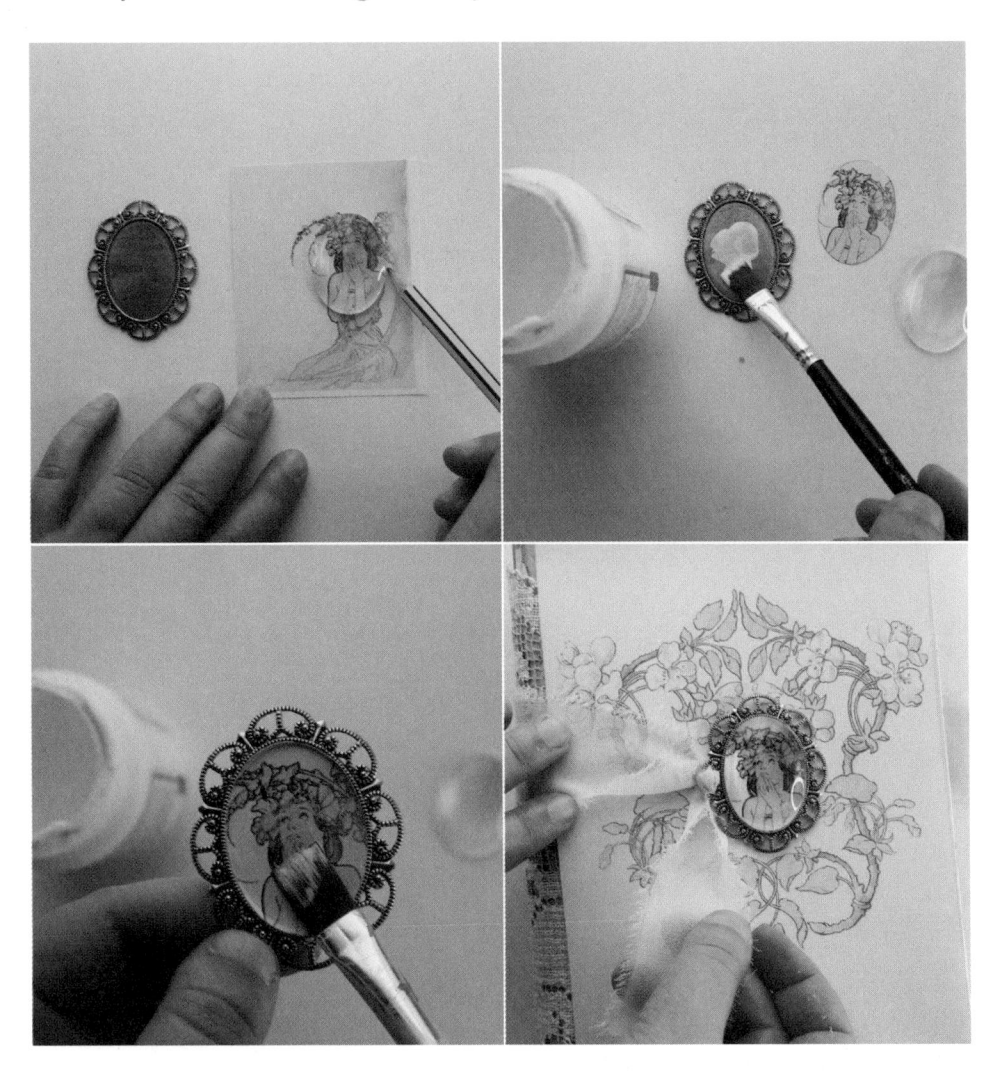

To wrap up the journal, you can use a ribbon and a cameo. To match the theme, you can cut a piece from a digital image that you like and then apply it with a little amount of Mod Podge. Apply another thin coat on top, and then place the glass on it. Thread the ribbon through the side spaces of the cameo, and that's it. Simple but effective!

CHAPTER 13

How to Create a Pouch Junk Journal

This journal came out of one of those moments when I reflected on how to use the items that I had collected. I knew that this bag had potential! To avoid the risk of making my house cluttered, I usefully set a deadline for which, if I didn't use the recycled item by then, I would give it away. And this bag was dangerously near it; also, at the time of writing this book, I was in the middle of moving and the last thing I needed to do was also move my collection of "junk."

So here is a journal in which we can take advantage of the natural shape of the bag, without cutting it. It's perfect to store your scraps, stickers, or stationery.

Tools and Materials

Recycled bag that you like
Some paper that you like, folded in half; for example scrapbooking paper, magazine pages, wrapping paper, etc., the same size as your bag (I'm using big A3 tea-dyed papers and digitals from TaylorMadeJournals)
360-degree rotating stapler or a ribbon to bind the pages together
Scissors
Acetate vinyl glue (like Fabri-Tac or Flash Bond)
Sari silk or a ribbon that you like for the closure
A bundle of pieces that you like (postcards, photos, papers) for final touches

Step 1: Adding the Pages to the Bag

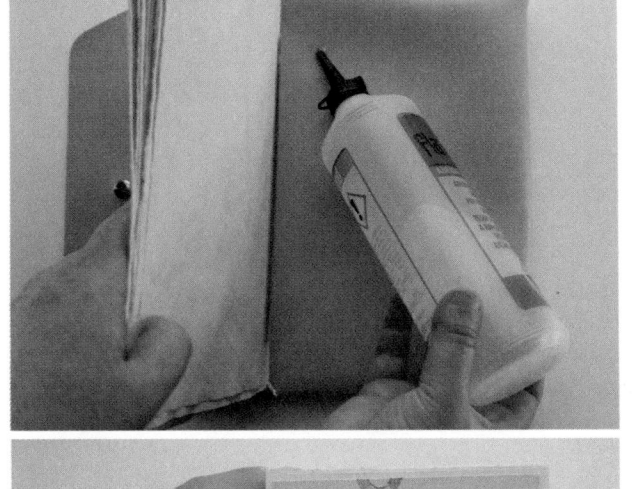

First of all, prepare a bunch of paper that you like and bind the sheets together with a stapler (like I showed you in a previous chapter), or use a ribbon. Glue the final page to the back of the bag.

Step 2: Embellishing the Front

Then take advantage of the natural belly band of the bag and clip a bunch of paper sheets layered one on top of the other. If there is no grip, glue it down. Use a ribbon to close the bag. Finally, you can add some more embellishments, like postcards, dried flowers, black-and-white photos, gold die-cut, etc. So now the bag is embellished and you can use the zip pouch for your scraps, ready to be used for a collage session!

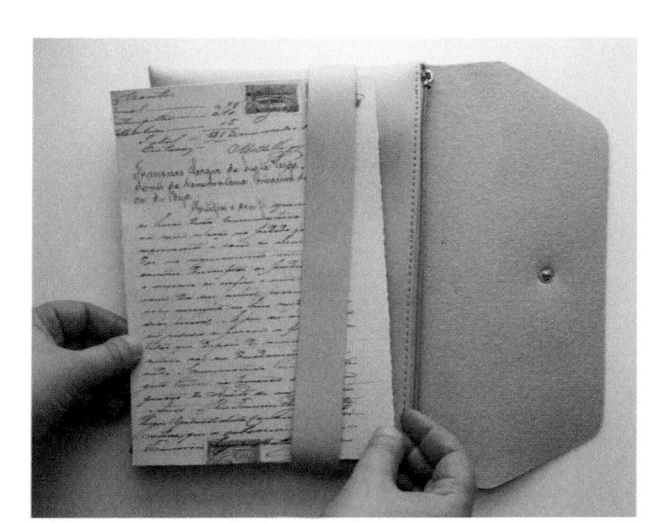

CHAPTER 14

How to Create a Junk Journal from a Plastic Bag

This journal is fun, easy to make, and…transparent! The idea for this journal came while I was unboxing the camera that I'm currently using for the pictures of this book. I was putting it in my special basket where I have all my things to recycle, and it landed on a scarf. And then something clicked! So here's my first experiment, and I'm glad to be able to share it with you.

Tools and Materials

A pluriball (bubble wrap) plastic bag (or a padded junk mailer)

Recycled scarf or some semi-transparent fabric

Scissors

Acetate vinyl glue (like Fabri-Tac or Flash Bond) + an old flat brush or an old credit card

Some paper that you like, folded in half; for example, scrapbooking paper, magazine pages, wrapping paper, etc.

Sari silk or a ribbon that you like for the binding

Step 1: Creating the Cover

Place your plastic bubble bag on a recycled scarf with a design that you like. Use scissors to cut a piece of scarf fabric the same size as the bag. Glue it down with a thin layer of acetate vinyl glue (to avoid stains). You can spread it with your fingertip, with an old, damaged flat brush (or be sure to wash it right after you've used it with dish soap and water), or with an old credit card. I love the transparency! I don't mind that the plastic is still visible on the back, but if you don't like it, cover it with something that you do like. I suggest you use something you like on both sides, because it will be a little visible through the plastic.

Step 2: Embellishing the Spine

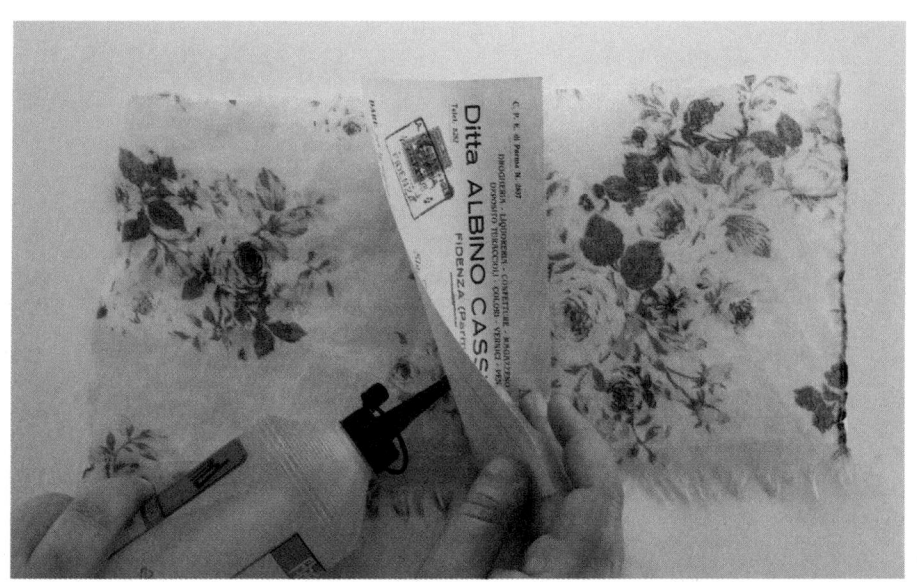

Use a piece of paper you like to cover the spine. I'm using a vintage Italian recipe.

Step 3: Adding the Pages

To add the pages, just use a ribbon that you like and pass it through the middle of the pages and outside the cover.

PUNCH, OR THE LONDON CHARIVARI. [MARCH 17, 1909.

Mr. TUCKWELL as the work of HAWKINS when Provost of Oriel.

HERE IN MY HEART

CHAPTER 15

How to Create a Junk Journal Folder

I'm a big fan of junk journals made without binding. This version that I'm going to share with you is very easy and fast to create. But the thing that I love the most is that it is made in a way that you can always adapt based on your needs. For example, I like to use large sheets to create color studies, swatch materials, create different versions of the same subject when I draw, mood boards, vision boards, and so on. The thing is that I usually prefer using a cheap sketchbook for that—the uglier the better, because I don't have to worry about how my experiments will turn out. If I mess things up, I'm not ruining anything! But, at the same time, I like to practice in my beautiful journals, the ones with all the vintage ephemera and beautiful trims too. But with time, I notice that I have a tendency to only write in those journals, instead of playing. In a sort of way, they are limiting me sometimes. So here is how I resolve that problem: creating a journal where I can combine beauty with the practical. With this journal, you can store loose pages and bind only the ones you like the most *after* practicing on them. The cover will be like an expandable folder, adaptable to your needs as you go. Alternatively, you can bind some pages right now and then add more in the future. You also can combine what you have already learned with some of these techniques. The possibilities are endless! I suggest playing and seeing what works for you. Push your boundaries, think with your head. Let's start!

Tools and Materials

Some paper that you like, folded in half (for example, scrapbooking paper, magazine pages, wrapping paper, etc.—I'm using tea-stained A3 sheets)

A piece of fabric you like to create hinges (I'm using a piece of recycled cotton), or use some masking tape plus washi tape, or simple scraps of paper plus glue

Scissors

Acetate vinyl glue (like Fabri-Tac or Flash Bond)

A vintage paper or a pattern paper that you like for the cover, a little smaller than the other pages

A piece of fabric that you like for the cover

Two pieces of cardboard or two pieces of a cover from a recycled book

A vintage letter or postcards, or something like that, for embellishing the cover (optional)

Sari silk or a ribbon that you like for the closure

Step 1: Binding With Hinges

Prepare some sheets that you like in the size that you want and fold them in half. I'm using ten tea-stained A3 sheets. The choice of the paper here depends on what you are going to use this journal for. And, more generally, what do you want? For example, I'll use this journal for experiments. I already know that I will use some materials that are not exactly made to be used on the paper that I'm using. For example, I recently got some new paints and I want to play with them. Probably this is not the best paper to try them on, but who knows! Maybe I will discover something new! Also, perhaps discovering what *not* to do from direct experience is sometimes more impactful and fun than learning it from someone else (as long as it's safe, of course).

You can place all your pages one on another and stop there, or bind them right now.

Cut a little of the fabric you have chosen and then tear it. Place the strip between two pages and use acetate vinyl glue to hold them together. Repeat this process with the other pages.

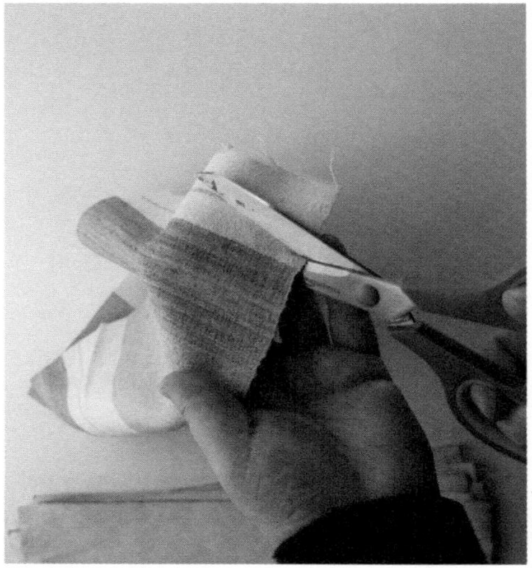

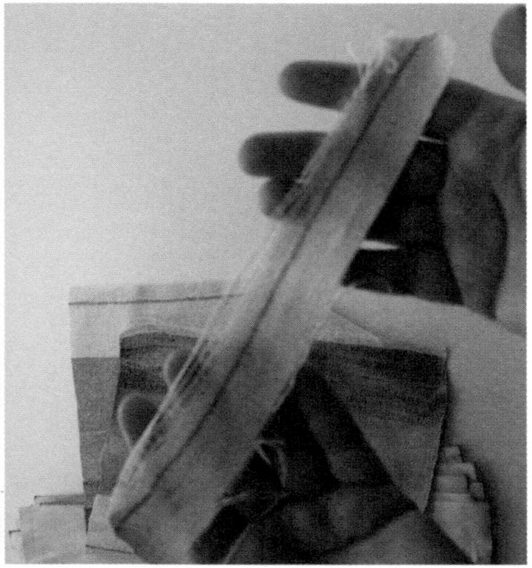

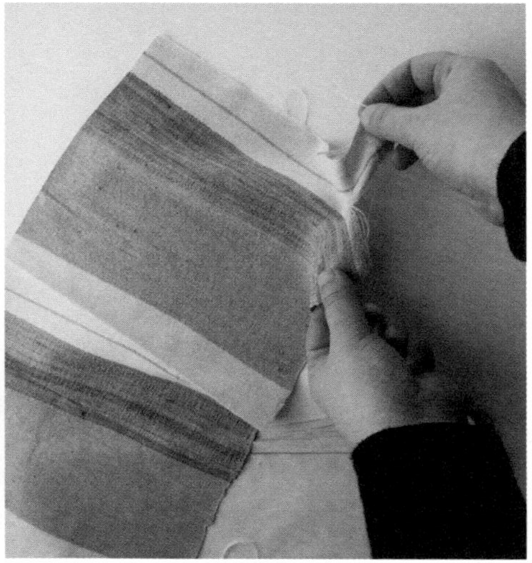

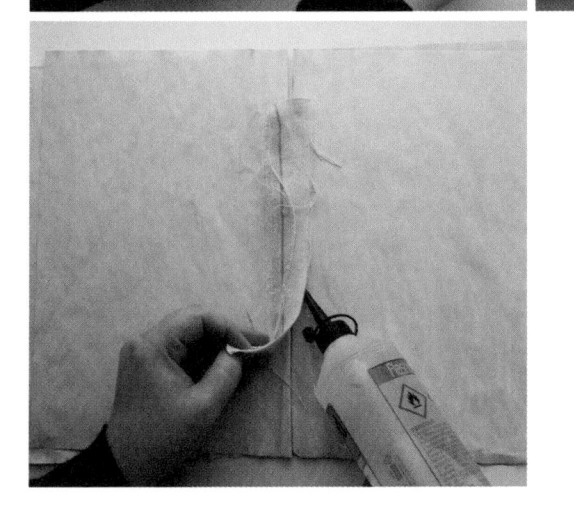

Step 2: Creating the Cover

Place a sheet of paper that you like on the pages you have created. I'm using a vintage piece from a newspaper, but you can use a vintage-style reproduction or something you like from a magazine. Glue a piece of fabric on that. Be sure that the fabric is long enough to contain all the pages and more.

At this point, glue a piece of cardboard onto the fabric and the page. I'm using an old cover from a book that I have recycled. To embellish, add some vintage paper or something you like on the top. You can do the same for the back, or leave the fabric loose. To hold everything together, use a sari silk ribbon or something you like. To create a little contrast, I have used a red one.

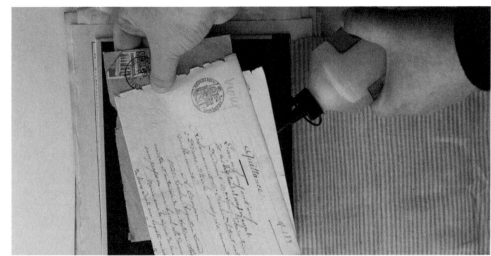

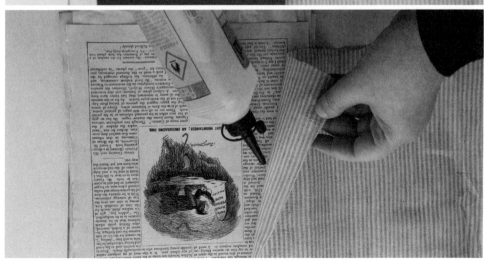

PART 3

How to Use a Junk Journal for Self-Care

CHAPTER 16

Art Journaling for Well-Being

Imagine a world where you can try new things without any judgment and just have fun with your journal. Experiment with it, invite magic into your world, and get relaxed in a secret, private place where you can create some time just for yourself, recharge your batteries, and express yourself in the most raw and authentic way.

This kind of place might feel like Wonderland, but there are people in the real world who seem to carry on with this incredible ability to be like Alice, and I was not one of them.

I was in primary school one day when the teacher let us play with some markers. I painted my whole face. Not the blank sheet of paper it was intended for…my face! Because I didn't know any better, I was curious, and I wanted to experiment. I just did it. And while I was painting, I felt so much joy, and I thought that I was doing an amazing job.

But then, when the teacher noticed it, she descended on me, yanked me out of my seat, and took me in front of a mirror and said: "Your face will never be the same again! Look! You ruined yourself!"

Then she left me there alone for hours, waiting for my mom to pick me up at school and show her what a mess I'd made. But when my mom came to get me, she consoled me and helped me clean up. She even laughed!

But I lost my magic for a long time after that. When I got older, I always felt an undertone of the fear of judgment when I was creating something. I was always thinking, "Is this allowed? Is this okay? Is this offensive to someone?"

I was always questioning my decisions. Until 2020, when the world went crazy with what we know and all of a sudden, everything seemed so meaningless. It was then that

I found all these artists on the web, using art as an adventure to better understand the reality of expressing feelings, and I wanted to be a part of it.

Then a whisper in my head recurred: *You are not an artist, you didn't study art so you can't do it, you are too old to start right now, you don't have time, and taking time just for you is selfish*…but then I came across an old photo of me as a toddler. And watching my old self, I realized that the inner critic in my head was not exactly me. The voice was made up of my old teacher and all the negative voices that had conditioned me over the years…so I asked my inner child: *What happened to you?*

I lost her because I wanted to be accepted. I wanted to be loved. But at what cost? I made other people's needs and beliefs more important than mine. How could I tolerate saying those cruel words to myself? *Is it too late? Is there no chance for her? Is she not worthy?* And my initial answer was no, and I started to cry. And I concluded that I respected myself enough, I cared about myself enough, to create some time just for me during the day. To try to change that answer.

And so can you.

I started with one hour on the weekend, and now it is every morning before life for the others begins, when everything is still silent. It can be five or fifteen minutes, it doesn't matter, the only idea is that I'm alone with my creative practice; this makes me feel unconditional love, and as if I'm living my life more intentionally. Every day, I show up as I am, and I know that with this practice, I'll set the mood for the entire day. It's so good that now I can't get enough!

Some call it the golden hour or sacred space, it's a sort of revisited "miracle morning." For me, it is like a date with myself.

Not everybody is an early bird, and I remember that, when I was in my teen years, my golden hour was at eleven p.m. So if you don't have a practice like this and you want to try, see what works for you. Maybe you are more like a night owl. Once Daniel Pennac said this about reading as a hobby: "Time to read is always time stolen." I would say that "time passed doing our craft is time created." And it is so precious and important that creating this time for us is a duty first of all, and then, a pleasure. Pause, breathe, and move your body. Pour a cup of tea. Playing with paper and glue, a five-minute sketch, slowly stitching a piece of fabric… Everything can be put in a journal, one little project at a time. Making something with our hands and journaling forces us to slow down and meditate on our lives.

Expressing and understanding ourselves and our environment is the basis for living more in alignment with our true values, making decisions, and acting according to what we truly believe and want. When this happens, we are more grounded, calm, and happy. And who doesn't want peaceful and happy people around?

Especially during challenging times, being able to remain grounded can make a huge difference in the way we approach life. For me, the purpose of creating visual pages by journaling is to facilitate the emergence of emotions that are suppressed and stuck somewhere in my body and in my unconscious for many reasons. It can be the anxiety of trying to please others except me, to be accepted and loved. It could be the hopelessness in a society conditioning you, for example, that a kind of dream is impossible at your age, you name it. All kinds of limiting beliefs can be there, things that others put in our minds. These types of things are suffocating and repressing our true self, the self that we are when we come into this life.

To be fair, these are coping mechanisms that a part of us uses to keep us safe. Sometimes we do what we do just to be sure we'll remain in the group. The thing is, sometimes it's too much. The key word here is "balance." Another key word is "discernment." We have to train our critical thinking and listen and test our intuitions.

We are social animals, and to be a part of the community, we have to follow some rules, but at the same time, we have to know our true values, which are not necessarily the values of the society, and be conscious of that when we act. One thing that stuck with me all these years from my studies in psychology is this: people are proud of themselves and happy when they act in alignment with their true values. When our actions are the reflections of what we think is right to do. To be clear, it takes a lot of courage sometimes—it's simple, but not easy.

Nonetheless, we live in a world of constant propaganda, TV, and social media; everybody is selling something. It can be a product or an idea, and it seems that whoever makes the most noise wins. And if it's free, remember that you are paying with something else.

To lift the veil of this chaos, we have to shut down the external stimuli. When everything is quiet, we can start to listen to things from within and be more lucid.

It's like being at a restaurant: it could be the most fantastic restaurant in the world, but if we eat fast, without savoring the food…it's like eating junk food, there is no difference. And the experience is not that great. But when we eat and do nothing else…the food will be tasty. The same for a lunch with simple food: if we give it the right importance, without a TV in the background or other noises…even a simple piece of bread will taste better, because we will *taste* it.

Have you ever finished eating lunch and not realized you had eaten? Or have you ever driven to work and not realized you had driven? This is the autopilot that is living our life.

It's a normal process of automatization that helps us do things more efficiently and faster. But better? Not always. When we have to escape from danger, it's common to not consciously think about every part of how we have to drive a car. But being constantly a zombie in front of a screen is not good.

Balance is always the key for me. Be aware and consciously decide what is good.

So sometimes it's okay to step back and take some time to reflect on how things are going, and whether they are the things that I want in my life or not. To live life, change things where it's possible, and accept it when it's not, but never be passive, watching your life go by. It can take us only five minutes or one hour a day; you have nothing to lose, and everything to gain.

A good method to overcome autopilot is journaling—especially using images to create a journal page. That's because images are symbols and are a visual representation of an idea. It's better than a hundred words because they are a primitive stage of being; images are before words. We can communicate with images in a second. With images, we can express a feeling without trying so hard with words. Words come after. Images are symbols that speak in a language that we can understand before understanding. It's felt before thinking. And it's a great way to go deeper and discover aspects of ourselves in the shadows. And release stuck emotions. Emotions are energy in motion; they have to flow, not be stuck. And sometimes processing them hurts in the moment, but then we feel better. Have you ever heard someone say, "You need a good cry"? A hug and a hot cup of tea complete the magic. We feel better after we release a weight.

Our journal is a safe place to deal with release.

Where can we find these shared images? The psychoanalyst Carl Jung would have said, in the "collective unconscious." They are within us from when we are born.

Some ideas, concepts, and images are recognizable to everybody. Jung called them "archetypes." They are groups of patterns that represent the same universal symbolism.

When we recognize ourselves in the archetypes, we feel understood and less alone. When we understand, we can heal our wounds and break the toxic patterns of our lives that don't serve us anymore.

When does this identification emerge? When can we trigger our hidden emotions?

One way is when we listen to a song and we get emotional for apparently no reason. For me, it came a lot when I was a teenager, listening to Alice in Chains, and now when I cry listening to Sigur Ros: even if I don't understand the lyrics, I *feel* the lyrics.

For some people, it works the same when they look at a painting, on the wall, or in a deck of cards. It works for everyone when we see a good film, or we read a good book, and we identify ourselves in the journey of the hero.

These are all good ways to feel our feelings in a safe place. And then we can capture them to digest them in our journal, like we are talking to a friend who never gets bored listening. It's a supportive practice, it's to train ourselves to be comfortable in the momentary discomfort, and so become stronger or be able to see better opportunities.

For example, years ago, I was in a very bad job environment. It took months to admit to myself that all I had constructed was based on a weak foundation. It was painful to look at the truth, but then I found another job, and I couldn't stop thinking about why I hadn't acted earlier. Sometimes we cling to illusory certainties and we trade our freedom for false security. Through journaling (and other things), I understood that I was not changing because I invested in it for so long! I didn't want to quit and consequently feel "stupid." The worst part is that I was doing it all by myself, no one was forcing me.

I "just" had to recognize that I was not a victim of the circumstances, and that I could change.

Would you believe that even my face's shape had literally changed? Maybe we can unconsciously lie to our minds, but the truth will always be revealed through our bodies, in my opinion.

When I finally changed jobs, I looked ten years younger! Of course, because I released suppressed tension and my sleep had improved. From that, I've learned a lesson: cut the losses when it's time, embrace shame or whatever with a lot of compassion, and move on.

So I hope that journaling will be a reliable tool in your discovery journey, as it is for me. There are a lot of ways to do it; some are more passive and some are more "active." Let's explore what works for me, and may this be inspiring for you too in your practice.

Creative Visual Journaling

This is a guided method to help you unlock your intuition. Coming from a psychological background, for me, it's natural to create my pages inspired by what's come from my mind along the way—it's like a conversation "between me and me," unfolded on the page, that comes to life. My art journal is a co-creator itself, and it could be the same for you; just try and see if this could be your cup of tea. The fun part is that, usually, at the end of this process, there is a message from the page! Let's find out together!

Step 1: Preparing Yourself

To speak with your subconscious, you have to set the mood. Light a candle to give importance to this moment, or make some tea just for you. You deserve a moment of quiet. Try to accept the little discomfort of staying in silence, if this emerges, without distractions all around. For example, turn your phone to airplane mode and create your space in the morning, when everybody is still sleeping and everything is quiet. The light represents your intention to understand yourself better and give yourself a moment of unconditional love. The magic is not in the candle itself, it's in the focus of your intention. This is a practice of acceptance. When you accept yourself as a whole, good and bad, and everything in between, then you can be happier and eventually grow and respond better to the circumstances of the world.

When we are aware and lucid, we can stop reacting and start responding proactively. We stop living on autopilot, making the same mistakes over and over, and begin to notice why we do what we do, accept our flaws, embrace discomfort, and give ourselves love. The kind of love that a good parent can give us. The difference is that, in this case, we can give ourselves that kind of love. In psychology, it's called "reparenting." Do research on this topic if you want to go deeper; on the internet, there's a ton of free material that you can use.

Step 2: Brainstorming

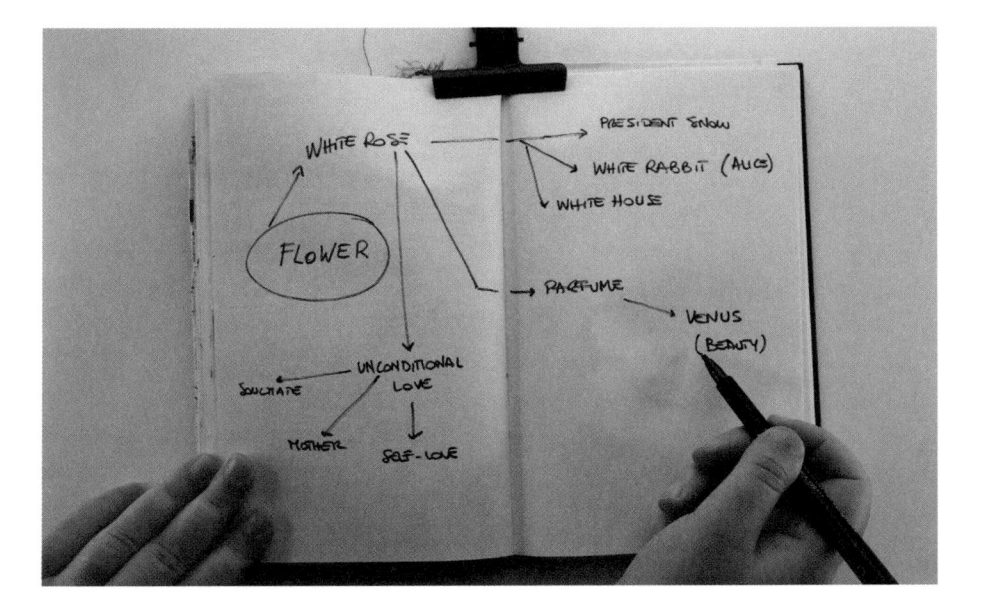

I have a "secret" sketchbook that I use to record all my experiments with paints, mixed media, work in progress, etc. I purchased it very cheap, and it's just meant to be for me; that's why it's so liberating to use it for some brainstorming at the beginning of a project. When you warm up in something that's not precious, you don't have a fear of ruining the pages, and you are free to make mistakes more than usual. Energy begins to flow easily in this way. Just start and trust in the process. Motivation and inspiration will follow.

If you have one, take it out right now, or you can use a normal sheet of paper. Write down a simple word in the middle: for example, "flower."

This is one of my favorite prompts that I use again and again because, with this method, the outcome will always be different. Let me explain why: you can have the same starting point, but you will always be in a different moment of your life when you use it. So the outcome will be different, no matter what, because we change with time, it's inevitable. The good thing is that you can explore the same theme over and over at different times of your life, and then confront your pages and reflect on what has changed. This is a method to create some distance in the stories of your life and have a better perspective. It's like going to the top of a mountain and observing from a distance the town below. It's like seeing things from the outside.

The prompt "flower" is also one of my favorites because it is versatile and very easy and inspiring to use. You don't need to change the prompt every time you journal. Choose something that you are passionate about, and you'll see that your journal gets filled only with that single sparkle!

If you don't come up with anything different right now, try "flower" as a prompt, just to test this process. Then you can take only what resonates and feel better, and then integrate that part with your practice to create something unique that works for you.

Flowers have beautiful colors, smell good, and make everybody happy, don't they? And they have meanings! You can explore so many things starting from this!

So, as I was saying, start by writing the word "flower" in the middle of your page.

From that, note everything that comes to your mind on the paper.

The goal here is to avoid censorship and get messy; the weirder, the better! It's very similar to the process known as "automatic writing" described by Julia Cameron as "morning pages" in her book *The Artist's Way* (highly recommended). It's a sort of loose version of the "free associations" invented by Sigmund Freud. The difference is that we are alone with our journal, and we are using mind mapping to follow the links that our mind is creating. Ask yourself, for instance, what is your favorite flower. Why? What's the meaning? Does your city have a particular flower in its flag that is representative or very common? Are you named after a flower? Maybe someone you know has a floral name with a significant meaning. What is the color of this flower? What's the meaning behind that color in your culture? Is there a myth or a story about this? A planetary association? Write everything, drawing bubbles with connections, or simple words linked by lines. This mind map will help a story to emerge from within you, that maybe is craving to be told. For instance, for me, the first thing that came up was "the white roses," the first gift that my soulmate gave to me.

Write all the emotions that are coming and try to notice what you are feeling through your body (for example, for me in this case, it was warmth in my chest). This will help you to release what has to go out and claim what empowers you, like some desire and actions that you can take today to feel better (for example, for me, it's something like, "I'm grateful for the love of my family, I want to spend more quality time with them").

Write also how you can represent physically what is unfolding (for example, for me: colored and black-and-white photos of the first white roses that my soulmate gifted to me, the lyrics from songs about roses, President Snow and his white roses from *The Hunger Games*, the white rabbit from *Alice in Wonderland*, the planet of beauty, Venus, white cloths from my mom, a perfume that I have that smells like roses, the White House, etc.).

If something does not make sense in this phase, it's totally normal.

Step 3: Choosing Ideas

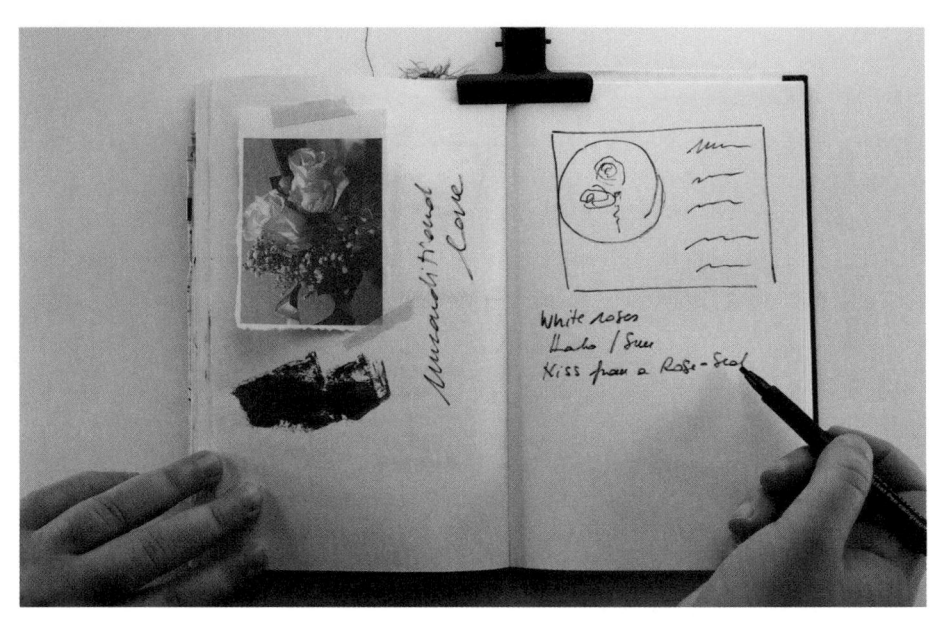

Take what resonates the most and choose what fits better in the narrative that is coming alive. Gather materials that represent your ideas in physical form. For instance, for me, those were: the white roses print in black and white, the lyrics from the song "Kiss From a Rose" by Seal (that is a gentle song that evokes calm in me), my favorite perfume, which smells like roses (that relaxes me), and a bronze/gold acrylic paint to use. The idea that is coming and that I want to represent is that I'm grateful for the unconditional love that I have in my life (represented by the rose and the white). Important thing: choose what makes sense for you; nobody has to see your page unless you want them to. When you see the page in the future, it will be a key that opens the doors to unique stories and feelings and everything in a second. That's why I call them "key symbols." That's the power of images, images that come from you. That's why I like to use personal symbols that have a particular meaning for me, not only the universal ones. For example, for me, the "white roses" has a universal meaning of a "pure love relationship," but at the same time, it is the symbol of self-love and self-respect that, when it's there, also shines a light for others.

Step 4: Ideas for Composition

Choose the page you want to work with. I opened the art journal that we made together in the previous chapter, and I found that the first page on the left is perfect. So I changed my initial plan to create a spread of two pages, and instead, I will complete what I have already initiated.

So now you can start playing with the elements you've chosen intuitively, noticing what you like as you move all your elements through the page. Usually, what works is, for example, using the "rule of thirds" that consists of dividing the page with guidelines. You can find them, for example, on your phone camera by activating the "grid" tool in the settings section. Point your photo camera with the grid on and observe through the lens. Where the lines touch, that is where it's better to put your focal point. A simple way to use the rule of thirds loosely is to place the main object of interest away from the center (the opposite of children's drawings, if you think about it). I think it's always good to know some rules, to have more tools and possibilities to express better what we want to express through our art, but in this case, it's not the most important thing. My advice is to follow this tip if you feel lost and if you want to be more confident and surer of creating something balanced and harmonious, but at the same time, feel free also to do what feels right in your gut at that moment.

In this instance, it is more important to unlock something that is inside us than to make pretty pages, in my opinion. And of course, one thing does not exclude the other. In my case, I can put the photo in the center because it's an image with elements inside, one that has already a good composition because of the subject: it's a bouquet made by a professional florist. So you can see that the composition works because it's made by a designer who knows what she is doing.

So here's another tip: if you are not familiar with composition and you are afraid to start, use images of art in every form in your journal. You can learn a lot! For example, you can notice in my case, how my roses are making a sort of "big C," and your eye starts moving from the top to the bottom in a natural, smooth way because of the little flower filler all around that is useful as a gentle background. Also note the little heart that balances the fact that the roses are only two and too far to the left.

If you look at this photo through the grid of your phone, you'll notice that the roses touch one of the candidates for the ideal place for a focal point. The only thing that I want to add is more difference in light and shadow, to add some depth.

Anyway, note what you like about your composition in your sketchbook and make some thumbnails to see which composition you like best. Play and have fun!

Step 5: If You Feel Stuck

At some point, it is perfectly normal to feel stuck or have a bad feeling about your project. It can be some sort of resistance, insecurity, you name it. Knowing that everybody, from the beginner to the most revered artist, goes through this stage is encouraging. We are not the only ones who go through the ugly stage of a project! Here are some pieces of advice; try them and keep in mind that we are all different, so explore what works for you.

Distance yourself from your work: for example, go for a walk, and remember to always treat yourself with compassion (I took a walk and bought myself some flowers at the market, for example). Reflect on what comes from it, and how you feel, and write about it. Add ideas, connections, and new epiphanies (if they come) on the first brainstorming/ mind map page. It doesn't matter whether we will use them or not, the important thing is to let them emerge and flow, so that we can process and then release them. You can always reuse some ideas in future projects.

At the end of this stage, you'll have ideas to express your story through the five senses (in my case, I have a beautiful song in mind to listen to and inspiring quotes from it, rose perfume to smell that reminds me happy moments, meaningful photos to see, and eventually, cozy fabrics to touch and add).

Step 6: Selecting Elements to Work With

I chose the photo in black and white because it represents a precise moment from the past (a date with my soulmate). In films, when there are flashbacks, they are sometimes in black and white; the same goes for old photos. So it's easier to associate past events with muted colors (and there's something elegant and precious about black-and-white photos, isn't there?). I glued it down and then covered the page with some clear gesso to have a nicely gripping primer for the paint that I'm going to use. It's not necessary, but it's better. It's like makeup: if you use a primer for your face, the foundation will apply better on your skin.

I decided to use bronze paint all around to create depth.

This is inspired by medieval paintings that have golden auras behind their subjects, especially saints. So for me, instead of using the idea of Venus, I will use the idea of having a sun behind the roses because it's a symbol of something sacred, important, and at the same time, something that gives me the sensation of nourishment, protection, strength, and joy. This way, I have a sort of yin (the rose that receives) and a yang (the sun that gives). I could continue for hours to search for or invent meanings! For me, it's fun.

As I said before, this makes sense to me, and it's okay if you don't see what I see. It's just to give you an example of my experience and tell you that it's okay if your page makes sense only for you. If others see the same things, well, better, but it is not necessary in this case, because the goal is to do something for you. When you create your page, you are projecting on paper something from within you. It's yours.

It doesn't have to be so deep every time, and it's easier and faster to do it than to explain it. It just gives you an idea of what you can create with a few elements, and what you can achieve: a page that speaks to you from you. It's a portal to your soul.

To make the "halo"/sunlight, you can use a plastic box cover as a template (useful because you can see through it and so you can regulate where your circle has to be). With a brush dipped in gold or bronze acrylic paint, go over the circle and, once it is dried, repeat, moving the template a little. Clean your brush with water right away when you are finished, or it will turn hard and be ruined.

Notice that I changed some of the initial ideas: I like the not-fully-painted circle, so I left it as it was. There's no need to have big reasons to change things; it happens, so just go with the flow. Change things following your intuition as it emerges, it's fine.

Sometimes your collage will not make sense right away, or ever. As Sigmund Freud said, "Sometimes a cigar is just a cigar." And it's fine to play with paper just to play. But occasionally there will be a message, months later, when you are ready to listen to it. I think it's fascinating, magical, and contains a comforting healing power. And for me, that's my favorite thing. What will yours be?

Step 7: Connecting the Dots

You can add some elements here and there and journal about what comes into your mind. I added some tickets and stamps and a little piece of paper with my reflection. In the end, I didn't use the lyrics from a song, because I was inspired to write something spontaneously. But it's okay, our journal is in constant evolution, and that's so freeing!

The message that I got is something like, "Remember that family is your strength and they are always with you; give them the right importance." I love that!

I hope you enjoyed this demonstration of how I use art journaling for reflection, for understanding myself and the world around me, for living more consciously and not on autopilot…and definitely for releasing emotions. My wish is that it is useful for you too.

CHAPTER 17

How to Make Your Own Infinite List of Prompts

As I hope you have discovered in this book, there is no right or wrong way to journal. And there are a lot of ways to do it. In the last chapter, I showed you how I use creative journaling as a tool for self-reflection, as a way to have a conversation with my deepest self. But you can also simply be inspired by the thousands of prompts that you can find on the internet. You can also be inspired by a song, a film, a deck of cards, or a book. You can journal about your everyday life. But sometimes it might not be enough, and you could feel stuck, the fear of the blank page blocking you.

So in this chapter, I will give you a method to create your own infinite list of prompts. This will help you unfold your stories from within. In this way, you'll be able to expand your practice and you will be less dependent on external resources.

This method is inspired by the 5W of journalism. In fact, there is a rule that I learned when I was in school: when you are doing research, there are five questions that you have to ask. They start with the words who, what, why, where, and when. And I added a call to action (this last one is from my self-taught marketing studies).

Now take a category like "emotions" and/or "values." You can find a complete list by just searching "wheel of emotions" and "list of values" on the internet.

I choose these two categories because they are connected with our well-being (but feel free to use whatever you want). When we act in alignment with our values, we are good with our emotions. There are a lot of studies in psychology where it is demonstrated that a happy person is one who is coherent with his or her values. Corny example: if one of our values is *integrity*, we won't be happy if we earn money selling bad products.

So in a world where there is a strong disconnection from personal core values and society values, taking the time to slow down and reflect on what it really matters to *us* is a must, if we want to live life fully and intentionally.

Here's a short list of values and emotions that can be handy for you without searching on the internet.

Values

Wisdom, altruism, honesty, equality, balance, appreciation, acceptance, friendship, sustainability, adventure, independence, freedom, innovation, creativity, empathy, loyalty, compassion, achievement, authenticity, grace, beauty, courage, peace, etc.

Emotions/Feelings

Joy, happiness, love, anger, fear, envy, aliveness, awe, bliss, inspiration, pride, sadness, confidence, hurt, etc.

Let's Practice

Remember: set aside judgment and just write everything without censorship. Be specific. No one has to read your answers. Be like your best compassionate friend to yourself.

Choose one feeling or one value and cross it with the 5W. For example: we can choose joy (of course!).

Here's the list of prompts that we can come up with:

- Who brings joy to my life? Ex: my family, my friends…

  _____

  _____

- What makes me feel joy? Ex: spending quality time with my loved ones, baking a cake on a lazy Sunday morning, watching the light dance on my wall…

  _____

  _____

- When do I feel joy? When I wake up at home near my family, when we have a meal together…

  _____

  _____

- Where do I feel joy? Ex: at home, in nature…

  _____

  _____

- Why do I feel joy? Ex: because I feel mutual connection, belonging, and love.

  _____

  _____

Based on your answers to these questions, ask yourself:

- What is one little action that I can do today to bring more joy into my life? Create your call to action—"Call that family member who is far away today," for example—and stick with it.

_____

_____

_____

_____

Write everything that comes to your mind, the littler, the simpler, the better! Because if you find little things, it will be easier to create a call to action that you can really do right now.

Then you can draw, illustrate, add a photo or a picture from a magazine...or create a collage. All in theme with what comes out. There are a lot of ways in which you can express the thoughts and feelings that will emerge. Creativity used in this way can be a powerful tool to discover new things about yourself and elaborate new perspectives.

Let's practice with a "negative" emotion (notice: the reality is that there aren't good or bad emotions, just emotions, but it's natural that we tend to classify certain emotions negatively). Let me explain through an example: we can choose fear.

- Who makes me feel fear? Ex: Freddy Kruger, spiders…

_____

_____

- What makes me feel fear? Ex: making something new, losing agility…

_____

_____

- When do I feel fear? Ex: when I have to perform in some way (exams, job interviews, live on YouTube, etc.).

  _____

  _____

- Where do I feel fear? Ex: in a heavy-traffic area, at parties…

  _____

  _____

- Why do I feel fear? Ex: because I'm insecure, I'm afraid to say the wrong things and lose acceptance…

  _____

  _____

Based on your answers to these questions, ask yourself:

- What is one little action that I can do today to manage my fears more efficiently?

  _____

  _____

Fear is a signal that tells us that we want to protect ourselves from something. You see? It's not "bad" at all! So for me, a call to action could be "invite my neighbor for tea and embrace all the silly things that maybe I'll come up with" or "drive in that heavy-traffic area, but maybe not at rush hour." By doing this, we can create a small reminder that, to contain our fears, we "just" need to face them. It is better in small doses, of course.

Let's try it with a value.

For example, we can choose courage.

- Who is the person who comes up in my mind who has courage? Ex: my mom, Aisha Khan, Braveheart, Gandhi…

  _____

  _____

153

- What is courage for me? Ex: doing the right thing when there's no one watching, when there is no reward, encountering something that scares me and doing it anyway…

  _____

  _____

- When do I feel that I'm courageous? Ex: when I stand up for the right thing, when it's not trendy, when I defend someone from something…

  _____

  _____

- When do I feel courageous? Ex: on YouTube every time I post a new video…

  _____

  _____

- Why do I feel courageous? Ex: because I have fear but I do things anyway…

  _____

  _____

So what can I do to feel courageous today? For example, I can share my answers with you and be vulnerable, so maybe you'll feel more comfortable in trying this practice too.

Keep in mind that you don't have to create an answer to all these questions. You can always adapt this practice in whatever way you want. Just have fun!